AFFLICTED

AFFLICTED POWERS

Capital and Spectacle in a New Age of War

RETORT

Iain Boal, T. J. Clark
Joseph Matthews, Michael Watts

VERSO

London • New York

First published by Verso 2005
© Retort 2005
This edition published by Verso 2006
All rights reserved

3 5 7 9 10 8 6 4

Verso
UK: 6 Meard Street, London W1F 0EG
USA: 180 Varick Street, New York, NY 10014–4606
www.versobooks.com

Verso is the imprint of New Left Books

ISBN–13 978–1–84467–031–4
ISBN–10 1–84467–031–7

British Library Cataloguing in Publication Data
A catalogue record for this book is available from the British Library

Library of Congress Cataloging-in-Publication Data
A catalog record for this book is available from the Library of Congress

Typeset in Garamond
Printed in China by C&C Offset Printing Co., Ltd.

Frontispiece image, page vi:
Unidentified Iraqi (by some reports Detainee #18470)
under torture by US forces, Abu Ghraib prison, 2003.

In memory of
Michael Rogin
1937–2001

And reassembling our afflicted Powers,
Consult how we may henceforth most offend
Our Enemy, our own loss how repair,
How overcome this dire Calamity,
What reinforcement we may gain from Hope,
If not what resolution from despare.

Paradise Lost, Book 1

CONTENTS

PREFACE

Retort is a gathering of some thirty or forty antagonists of the present order of things, based for the past two decades in the San Francisco Bay Area. Four of the group – Iain Boal, T. J. Clark, Joseph Matthews, and Michael Watts – did the main work of writing *Afflicted Powers*. The book builds on Retort's broadsheet, *Neither Their War Nor Their Peace*, produced for distribution at the anti-war demonstrations in the spring of 2003.

A word on the book's form. After preparatory work by the four of us separately and together, each one of the quartet took responsibility for the first drafting of a chapter. Every paragraph was then subjected to scrutiny, discussion, and multiple revisions by all four. The book developed from a counterpoint of concerns, kinds of knowledge and forms of expertise, and in the end we made no attempt to produce a text with a singular voice or seamless style. We ask the reader's indulgence, therefore, for a certain shifting of focus and tone in what follows, confident that the conditions of the book's production contribute to, rather than detract from, *Afflicted Powers'* analytical force.

The book's stance is deliberately polemical, in the tradition (we hope) of the pamphleteering characteristic of the Left in its heyday. On occasion we turned aside in the course of our writing – for encouragement, but also to remind ourselves sadly of what once seemed possible – to read a few pages from Rosa Luxemburg's great *Junius Brochure* or Randolph Bourne's *The State*. And our chosen examples speak immediately to what we hope *Afflicted Powers* can achieve. Both the Bourne and the Luxemburg interventions were responses to the horrors of 1914–18. Both writers considered it an urgent necessity, in that worst of all moments, to think the phenomenon of war in relation to the capitalist state. Like Bourne and Luxemburg (though with no illusions about recapturing their inimitable coldness and rage), we believe that the new 1914 which confronts us demands in answer an interrogation of the very terms and forms of politics.

Following the example of the *Junius Brochure*, at points in the book certain arguments and assertions are made without resort to the formal critical apparatus of scholarship; footnotes there are few, the larger canvas of relevant literature largely invisible. At other points, the nature of the subject at hand demands a level of historical and empirical detail (even exegesis) in order for the book's criticism of the present to be sustained. In either circumstance, the point is to open a case, not nail it down. For readers who wish to explore further the issues that *Afflicted Powers* takes up, we provide some bibliographic landmarks and signposts in a brief Endnote. Retort may be reached directly at retort@sonic.net.

IB, TJC, JM, MW
Berkeley and San Francisco, November 2, 2004

INTRODUCTION

It bears repeating. On February 15, 2003, and again on March 15, with the first wave of bombing by that time a matter of hours away, millions of people took to the streets to voice their opposition to the oncoming invasion of Iraq. The marches began in Melbourne and Sydney, and swept westward with the sun. The centers of Rome, Tokyo, London, Paris, Madrid, Buenos Aires, Berlin, Dhaka, Barcelona, New York, San Francisco, and a thousand other communities were choked with banners and echoing with rejection and disgust. Believable estimates the day after put the number of demonstrators in February between fifteen and twenty million, maybe higher; even the networks and newspapers of record – desperate as ever to keep the Great Refusal off the front page – were not able to shrink the figure by more than a factor of two. The "embittered few" had become the disbelieving and contemptuous many.

In common with almost everyone, the writers of this book could hardly believe their eyes as they swung with the crowd into San Francisco's Market Street. Out of the torpor and humiliation of "politics" in Bush's America had come, abruptly, a foreshadowing of a different form of life. The crowd itself – the feeling was palpable at the time – seemed to shake its head, wide-eyed with astonishment, at the unlikeliness of its own coming into being. Where had this energy been sleeping? Why had the months-long combined operation of Republicans and Democrats, aimed at making opposition to empire unthinkable –

Photo: Martin Sasse/LAIF

Anti-War Demonstration, Baghdad, February 15, 2003

unrepresentable – so signally failed? How could it be that the idiom of the chants and placards, which for a moment made a world, had so unerringly decided on the proper form of reply to the predawn barrage of lies – a reply so apt and incisive, inflected so variously and yet so consistent in its venom? As if all of us had sat brooding nightly over CNN, rolling the latest sound bite round our tongues, savoring it, entering deep into its banality and untruth, until an *absolute negation* had emerged for each demonstrator, shadowing the official slogans, parodying them, feeding on their emptiness, giving them monstrous form.

We take such moments of elation seriously. They are rare, in our experience; and when they come, they provide the measure for the lockstep, souped-up simulacrum of enthusiasm on which the "I'm for Choice" normality of politics depends. This book issues from the actions of February and March. As we say in our preface, it builds on a broadsheet written by us for distribution at the two events. We should like to begin by insisting proudly, therefore (against the purposeful forgetting of all the organs of official history), on the unprecedented nature of the movement in the streets. It was a world-historical moment. Never before had such masses of people assembled, against the wishes of parties and states, *to attempt to stop a war before it began.* In the run-up to armed conflict, so history monotonously tells us, the state has its finest hour. Nothing is easier for it than to whip up an attack-dog unanimity, compounded of fear, aggressivity, and xenophobia. The great words come out of cold storage: tyranny, democracy, humanity, Terror, the national interest, the imminent danger, the civilized world. "Internationalists" discover a love of country. Dissenters become nonpersons. Maybe an occasional Edmund Burke speaks out: "It is not with much credulity I listen to any, when they speak evil of those they are going to plunder. I rather suspect that vices are feigned or exaggerated, when profit is looked for in their punishment. An enemy is a bad witness: a robber is a worse."[1] But by and large, at the moment of mobilization, and while the horror of the opening campaigns is unfolding, the enemies of war can do nothing but wait – for the slow drip of disillusion to bring citizens to their senses and the smell of corpses to seep into the Rose Garden.

It remains a great new fact of politics, then, that on this occasion the script of war was not followed: that in every corner of the imperial heartland political actors refused to believe what their warlords were telling them, and worked, unsuccessfully, to interrupt the course of events.

Unsuccessfully. Of course the proviso is bitter, and in a sense absolute; and every day now, as the horror in the Middle East deepens and the vanguard of jihadists gathers strength, the proviso becomes harder to bear. Elation is one thing, effectiveness another. "If not what resolution from despare … "

1 Edmund Burke, *Reflections on the Revolution in France*, Harmondsworth 1969 (first pub. 1790), p. 246.

*

What exactly the constellation of factors was that made the marches possible is, in our view, an open question. The sheer ponderousness and hypocrisy of the pre-war buildup – and its constant *visibility*, the repeated set-pieces of lying and bullying to the world at large – mattered a great deal. So did the momentum provided by the previous years of "anti-globalization" struggles in the streets, and the links these demonstrators had forged with the older peace movements. Much of the groundwork had been local, that is, the result of piecemeal organizing, carried out face to face. But clearly the marches had other, newer origins. We are prepared to accept, taking our cue from an optimistic strand of current theory, that one ingredient of the February and March dynamic was the appearance on the world stage of something like a digital "multitude", a worldwide virtual community, assembled (partly in the short term over the months of warmongering, and partly over the preceding decade, as various new patterns of resistance took advantage of cyberspace) in the interstices of the Net; and that some of the intensity of the moment derived from the experience of seeing – of hearing, feeling, facing up to – an *image* of refusal become a reality.[2] Maybe the new Spinozists have it right. Here at last was the multitude taking shape in the public sphere, already in possession of its own apparatus, by the look of it, its own spatiality, its own style; and perhaps what we saw as the days unfolded was a premonition of a politics to come.

But the multitude took shape and the leaders of the world ignored it: that is the point. *The multitude as a political force was born into – out of – the*

---

2 See Michael Hardt and Antonio Negri, *Empire*, Cambridge, MA 2000, and Hardt and Negri, *Multitude*, New York 2004. We borrow the term "multitude", which Hardt and Negri recover from Spinoza's political writings, to point to certain new possibilities of political assembly and reorganization opened up by cybertechnology. But in our view the same technology has also proved itself, over the past two decades, the perfect instrumentation of "spectacular" dispersal, isolation, and derealization – the machinery of a *self-administered* dreamworld. This dialectic (which is largely glossed over in Hardt and Negri's analysis) is something we return to repeatedly in what follows.

experience of defeat. The very moment at which its virtuality became – or sketched out – an agency in the chaos of statecraft was also the one in which it saw how little it could do. Or perhaps (and this is the hope on which the present book is founded) it was in defeat that the marchers gained a first intimation of how much it would take – what work of questioning and organizing, what constructing and discarding of new forms of action, forms of understanding, forms of alternative speech – for the "multitude" to be more than just another image-moment in a world of mirages.

We realize that political writing born of circumstances like these has a difficult balance to strike. The great phrase from Milton that provides us with our title – "And reassembling our afflicted Powers" – has, in our use of it, the problem written on its face. We make no excuse for turning the two last words of the phrase outward, and having them apply to the present powers that be. For part of the twenty-first-century situation is indeed the affliction of the previously invulnerable. The American empire lives in fear – partly factitious, partly justified by events – and the ways in which it has chosen to respond to that new condition over the past four years have led it, in Iraq, to something close to real strategic failure. (The defeat, if it happens, will be infinitely more damaging than that suffered thirty years ago in Vietnam; for it will register a failure to impose imperial will in a region that lies near the economic and geopolitical heart of things.) The affliction of Power, then, is a reality; and any attempt at a renewal of political thinking has to center on an account of its causes and phenomenology. But of course Milton's pronoun cannot be wished away. For *our* Powers too are afflicted. The state may be vulnerable, but the multitude has yet to learn how to take advantage of that weakness.

Much as we exulted in the insolence and dismissiveness of the counter-language on the streets in 2003, we were already haunted by its limits and insufficiencies. The placards spoke back to power – irrefutably – by aping

and warping the warmongers' truisms. So far so good. But to the extent
that a picture of wider and deeper causes emerged from the welter of signs
– and even an intimation of what else, in place of iPods and weapon-
systems, the multitude might propose as its positives – to that extent, the
marchers did little more than churn out truisms of their own. The alternative to war was Peace, we were told; and this seemed to be proposed not
just as an alternative (which might have been bearable, at least as a conceptual given), but as an answer, a specific countervailing force. The cause of
war was either the perfidy and dementia of rulers, or the crude imperative
of Oil. It was hard to remember on February 15 that one defining feature
of the political landscape during the previous decade had been the emergence – an unpredicted, unlikely emergence – of a worldwide opposition
to the new round of exploitation summed up in the word "globalization",
and that among the achievements of this opposition had been the entering
of the dread concept "capitalism" back into political speech. Oil now
displaced such clunky abstractions. A Bush demonology disguised the
great fact of complete party-political unanimity as to the nature (the necessity) of the War on Terror, the desirability of the Patriot Act, the
untouchability of Sharon's Israel, and the need for an end to Saddam.

Above all, we could detect no acknowledgement on the marches – and
by now you will recognize we are using "the marches" as synecdoche for
the whole pattern of resistance to the war and the regime over the past
four years – that the advent of al-Qaida had redrawn the political map.
It is one thing to recoil from the *uses* our masters have made of the
"threat". It is another not to recognize that the threat is real. Opposition
to the War on Terror, we believe, ought to begin by looking both enemies
– empire and jihad – square in the face, and underestimating the strength
and resilience of neither. Many a time in the past four years we have
called to mind the old Leninist boast of Che Guevara, that he and his
comrades would go on to make "ten, twenty, a hundred Vietnams". Little
did he dream what form the revolutionary vanguard would take in its

hour of triumph, and in whose name the hundred Vietnams would be fought. History is cruel, Allah is rarely merciful. But for those of us who have always regarded the notion of a militant, secretive, unicellular band of brothers, proprietors of Truth, representatives of the Chosen, makers (forcers) of the Future, as the deepest and most destructive illusion of the Left, there is a bitter aptness to the sight of a new vanguard striding the world stage – a horribly effective vanguard, given the goals it has set itself – whose Future is now declaredly the Past.[3]

You will see that the experience of February and March 2003 determines much of *Afflicted Powers'* substance. It dictates, largely, our choice of topics. We have tried, above all, to take the main propositions of the anti-war movement seriously: not to dismiss or reverse them, necessarily, but to see if they could be reconstructed in such a way as to have more specific purchase on the present. We end up pointing to various constituent features of the world of the single superpower – the nature of revolutionary Islam; the dynamics of a new round of capital accumulation; the entrapment of both empire and Terror in a battle of images; the extent to which war and the state are inseparable, mutually defining terms; the abiding (and deadly) attraction of the Leninist ideal – which we believe any future opposition will have to confront if it is to turn its spasmodic "We are Many" into a form (a practice) of politics.

This leads to the question of style – meaning imagined community of readers. For the advent of the multitude in the run-up to war did very much more than steer us toward a set of obligatory subjects. It determines our sense of what political writing may now aim to *be* – whom such writing can plausibly address, what tone it might adopt in present

---

3 This is far from our last word on the complexities of present-day Islamism, or even on al-Qaida. Most revivalisms turn out to be deeply in love with aspects of the present they claim to despise. But as a marker of what it is in al-Qaida's vision of agency and temporality that differentiates it from almost all previous forms of vanguardism, this first characterization can stand.

circumstances, what level of analytic detail deploy; in a word, how much and *how little* political writing can hope to do, in a social order dedicated to the end of discourse and the rule of entertainment. We are realists, which in the current situation equals pessimists most of the time. To put against the memory of the insolent multitude in February and March, with the image it proposes of a citizenry somehow immune to the surrounding cretinization, there is always as counterweight, festering at the back of our minds, Nietzsche's prophecy of the Last Man:

> The time has come for man to set himself a goal …. I say unto you: one must still have chaos in oneself to be able to give birth to a dancing star ….
>
> Alas, the time of the most despicable of men is coming, he that is no longer capable of despising himself. Behold, I show you the *Last Man*.
>
> "What is love? What is creation? What is longing? What is a star?" thus asks the Last Man, and he blinks ….
>
> Everybody wants the same, everybody is the same: whoever feels different goes voluntarily into a madhouse ….
>
> "We have invented happiness," say the Last Men, and they blink ….[4]

Or, worse still, Kojève's vision of the Final State:

> In the Final State there are naturally no more "human beings" in the sense of humans as makers of history. The healthy automata are satisfied (sports, art, eroticism, etc.), and the sick ones get locked up …. The tyrant becomes an administrator, a cog in the machine made by automata for others of their kind.[5]

---

4 Friedrich Nietzsche, *Thus Spoke Zarathustra*, trans. Walter Kaufmann, in *The Portable Nietzsche*, New York 1954, p. 129.
5 Alexandre Kojève to Leo Strauss, September 19, 1950, in Leo Strauss, *On Tyranny*, expanded edition, New York 1991, p. 255 (translation modified).

Too often, these days, these words seem to apply directly to the world around us.

We have been deliberately open – naively so, some will say – about the extent to which recent events have altered our sense of the possible. But the reader will find us moving, all through the following pages, between stubborn expectancy and unbudgeable sense of doom. The book returns constantly to its epigraph's "If not". That is to say, we are partisans of wishful thinking, provided the final recklessness and obstinacy are seen to issue – truly do issue – from an accounting of our Enemy, and a recognition of our loss.

Beyond these matters of style and subject matter lies the deeper question – the problem – of *Afflicted Powers'* preferred terms of analysis. "Capitalism", for instance, and "primitive accumulation". We take it the time is over when the mere mention of such categories consigned one – in the hip academy, especially – irrevocably to the past. The past has become the present again: this is the mark of the moment we are trying to understand. (It is "the end of Grand Narratives" and "the trap of totalization" and "the radical irreducibility of the political" which now seem like period items.) Nonetheless, there is a problem of vocabulary; which, as regularly with such problems, takes us to the very possibility of opposition – of real opposing speech – in the current situation. Whom do we think we are talking to, for instance, when (occasionally) we round on, or appeal to, something called "the Left"? What kind of fabulous survival do we have in mind here, and where do we think it is hiding out? Does it *read* any longer? And insofar as we hope for readers whose vision of politics is no longer premised on the Left–Right distinction, will they not immediately put our book back on the pile of new releases the moment they see the words "Capital and Spectacle" in our subtitle? Does not the first concept usher us back, however good our intentions, into the fantasy world of "final crisis" and "fundamental contradictions"? And is not the second the typical (obscure) totem of an ingroup?

We ask our readers to wait and see, essentially – to judge for themselves whether, in the body of the book, these new and old bearings allow us to navigate the present. But let us try to head off some obvious misunderstandings. We do not regard the set of economic forces and arrangements called "capitalism" as a magical shaping power, pulling the strings of everything in the world around us. We take it to be an indispensable term of analysis for much the same reasons as do the *Wall Street Journal* and the McCain–Feingold Act: because as a way of organizing the forces and relations of production capitalism possesses its own complex, but closely bounded, unity; because it has utterly vanquished all other ways; and because it has a preponderant, invasive influence – sometimes as crude as bribery and corruption, sometimes as imponderable as the character of the commodity-form – over the conduct of politics and the tempo and substance of culture. Not everything, however, needs to be traced to its source. Explanations are obliged to be vivid as well as plausible. To say that Osama bin Laden, for instance, is a phenomenon of capitalism because his money came originally from petrochemicals and his followers spend hours casing out Citicorp and the Prudential is not, yet, to speak to his specific character – his unwelcome power – as a revolutionary. With Cheney and Bush, the fit may be tighter. (But that too brings problems in its wake: it is one thing for an explanation to be vivid, another for it to be crushingly obvious. We tire of detectives solving crimes the criminals have never bothered to conceal.)

About "primitive accumulation" we can afford to be less circumspect. The last several years have seen, so most interested parties would agree, an extraordinary shift in the *means* by which the preponderant economic forces in the United States seem set to organize their next round of globalization. As recently as five years ago, proponents and opponents largely shared the view that the reshaping of the world economy then under way had come about, and would continue, as a result of "agreements" (meaning covert or overt fixing), unrestricted capital flows, dismantling of national controls and regulations (all democratically validated), cruelly imbalanced North–South terms of trade, cynical subsidy of the heartland's decrepit mills and plantations, and the continuing attentions of the World Bank and IMF. Far be it from us to say that this brutal apparatus is not still working full speed. But evidently in the late-1990s it began to cough and splutter; and for the past four years it has been supplemented, spectacularly, by a new resort to arms – a new round of conquest and colonization. We believe the words "primitive accumulation" are the right ones to describe what is happening, especially because the first word points to what is special (and for the Robert Reichs and Thomas Friedmans of this world, scandalous) about the new situation – the overtly "colonial" character of the war in the Middle East, and the nakedness with which the unfreedom of the free wage contract is now *placed back on the footing of sheer power, sheer forced dispossession.* Marx, when he coined the term "primitive accumulation", had in mind the long work of enclosure of the commons (and all its attendant migrations and criminalization) which had laid the ground for Britain's industrial revolution, by creating a mass of men and women with nothing to sell but their labor power. It is not clear that he realized to what extent the whole subsequent history of the world economy would go on depending, time after time, on renewed episodes of entrapment, displacement, crude rifling of resources, pitiless herding of the dispossessed into "company accommodation" and disease-ridden shantytowns – with views of the skyscraper cluster twenty miles away. We imagine poor Marx sitting opposite Paul Bremer on the flight from Washington to Baghdad in April 2003 (the idiocies of the new Chief Administrator on that occasion have entered journalistic folklore), listening to Bremer sermonizing the soldiers on the first priority of the occupation, in his view – the smashing of Saddam's state cartels and the immediate strong medicine of privatization. Private soft-drink factories, private armies, private sewage plants, private water systems, privatized hospitals politely turning the victims of bombing from their doors.

> These newly freed men became sellers of themselves only after they had been robbed of all their own means of production, and all the guarantees of existence afforded by the old … arrangements. And this history, the history of their expropriation, is written in the annals of mankind in letters of fire and blood.[6]

Sometimes the fires do no more than smolder. Lately they burn bright.

Some of our lexicon, then, we make no apology for. Some of it ("spectacle", for instance, "military neo-liberalism", "permanent war") we plan to define and defend as we go along. "Terror" and "terrorism" are unavoidable non-concepts, which we believe can be given a measure of cognitive force only gradually, as the book's whole picture of politics emerges. "Multitude", likewise, is a term we adopt partly hopefully, partly skeptically, expecting the reader to be similarly in two minds. *Something* is shifting in the technics and tactics of resistance – the anti-war marches are proof of that – but only a disabused look at al-Qaida's deployment of the same cyber-apparatus, and at the whole recent dynamic of spectacular politics, will let us decide if the "something" is smoke and mirrors or truly the beginning of a new offensive.

But the problem goes deeper than terminology. We know very well that other items in our vocabulary speak to insufficiencies – weaknesses – no work of theory can mend. Who *are* "we", anyway? (Not a power, not a nucleus, not a singularity; not, above all, an avant-garde. Four writers drawn from a thirty- or forty-strong occasional gathering of

---

6   Karl Marx, "The Secret of Primitive Accumulation", in *Capital*, vol. 1, Harmondsworth 1976 (first pub. 1867), p. 875.

kindred spirits; one of whom knows the hell of the Nigerian oil derricks first-hand, and another what it was like to practice law in the California prison system; one of us with Bruegel and Pasolini as his heroes, another the Levellers and Carlo Tresca.) Who are "we", and where do we stand in relation to the various possible oppositional identities we are constantly conjuring up – the peace movement, the multitude, the anti-capitalists (what a moment it was when *that* identity was suddenly common currency again, pronounced with a sneer by Lehrer and O'Reilly!), the Left, the progressives, the refuseniks, the assorted antino-mians, the mere "people on the streets"?

Some of the labels in this list we like more than others. "Antinomian", for instance, at least has the advantage of ushering us back into the seventeenth century, that great moment of crisis for the emerging modern state – the time of struggle, by part of the citizenry, "against Mammon", "against Moses and his Law", against all forms of clerisy and identity – and therefore the term seems strangely appropriate to the flavor of our present Holy Wars. But all the labels are weak: we make no bones about that. They are vague or nostalgic or vatically utopian. And it is above all this reality – a linguistic one, but ultimately much more than linguistic – which we try not to flinch from in what follows. We lack precise terms for the new energies, and we are painfully aware that a rela-tionship to them – a critical, practical, *theoretical* relationship, without the flavor of spokesmanship or the aftertrace of *redemption in thought* – remains to be made. It may even turn out that the term we are least willing to abandon in the process is the one we have lived with most skeptically for the longest time. The Left, the Left …

We each have our memories of the kind of work this word was called on to do in the militant's dismal peroration. It has earned too much of its present disrepute. And yet finally, strangely, we find ourselves unwilling to let the word go – to let it exit altogether from the stage of history. We know what comfort such surgery would give the Enemy (to bin Laden as much as to the hacks on Fox News), which has labored unceasingly through the centuries to put the concept out of bounds. It is an advantage to the term "Left", as we understand it, that it speaks from a moment of historical defeat: that it knows its own powerlessness in an age when battle is joined between two virulent mutations of the Right; that it keeps alive, in the face of all evidence to the contrary, the notion of an alternative to the capitalist order that will eventually *take advantage* of the great work of loosening and fragmentation and disenchantment that has been capitalism's central (appalling) achievement – take advantage of the great work, push it on to its revolutionary conclusion, propel it to a final paroxysm of uncenteredness and non-identity. However weak and compromised the term has become, then, the Left remains the name – the best name, the placeholder, the banner soaked in blood – for this last best hope of mankind.

Afflicted Powers aims above all to tackle what seems to us the distinctive feature of the new world situation: that is, its deep and perplexing doubleness. We find ourselves, quite suddenly, living in an age defined by a terrible atavism – a plunging backward into forms of ideological and geopolitical struggle that call to mind now the Scramble for Africa, now the Wars of Religion. But this brute return of the past is accompanied – here is the real challenge to understanding – by an equally monstrous political deployment of (and entrapment in) the apparatus of a modern, not to say hyper-modern, production of appearances. Interests and imagery collide. A bald-faced imperialism is crossed with a struggle for control of "information". Mistakes or overreach in the management of the image-world have immediate political consequences – as Aznar, for instance, discovered in the aftermath of the al-Qaida strikes on Madrid – and outright defeat in the war of appearance is something no present-day hegemon can tolerate. (This is our topic in Chapter 1.) If the Left is to survive as a political entity, it seems to us that its great (theoretical) task is to think this atavism and new-fangledness together, as interrelated aspects of the world system now emerging. We are all in need of sight lines in a new, and nightmarish, terrain. Facts are in order, as antidote to a world of half-truths; but so too are fresh concepts, or old concepts reworked mercilessly in the light of the present. The face of politics is changing. Its underlying bone structure may or may not be altering too. In either case, new descriptions are needed. *Afflicted Powers* is an effort to provide some.

Readers will find themselves shifting, in the chapters that follow, between hard and disagreeable materialities – cold figures of profit, piled-up statistics of death and impoverishment – and broadranging speculation on current forms of social control. This double perspective, to repeat, is true to the nature of the moment. And no one should leap to the conclusion that "materiality" in this case equals capitalism, whereas "spectacle" is a disembodied image-world, or a realm of inter-nalized (impalpable) representations. Spectacle is an exertion of social power. It does violence to human actors just as much as does the disci-pline of the production line. We shall return to this. Equally, in the formula "atavism and new-fangledness", readers should guard against leaping too readily to assign one or another element of the present situ-ation firmly to one or another category. New-fangledness does not equal spectacle. Atavism does not equal war, or al-Qaida. Our subject – if we were pressed to sum it up in an inevitably clunky phrase – is *the contradic-tions of military neo-liberalism under conditions of spectacle*. Distinguishing the old from the new in this hell is a task to test even Satan.

I

THE STATE, THE SPECTACLE, AND SEPTEMBER 11

He too fought under television for our place in the sun.

—Robert Lowell on Lieutenant Calley, 1971

We begin from the moment in February 2003, with the run-up to war in Iraq entering its final stages, when the copy of Picasso's *Guernica* hung in the anteroom to the UN Security Council Chamber was curtained over, at American insistence – not "an appropriate backdrop", it was explained, for official statements to the world media. The episode became an emblem. Many a placard on Piccadilly and Las Ramblas rang sardonic changes on Bush and the snorting bull. An emblem, yes – but, with the benefit of hindsight, emblematic of what? Of the state's relentless will to control the minutiae of appearance, as part of – essential to – its drive to war? Well, certainly. But in this case, did it get its way? Did not the boorishness of the effort at censorship prove counterproductive, eliciting the very haunting – by an imagery still capable of putting a face on the brutal abstraction of "shock and awe" – that the velcro covering was meant to put a stop to? And did not the whole incident speak above all to the state's *anxiety* as it tried to micromanage the means of symbolic production – as if it feared that every last detail of the derealized decor it had built for its citizens had the potential, at a time of crisis, to turn utterly against it?

These are the ambiguities, generalized to the whole conduct of war and politics over the past four years, that this chapter aims to explore. We start from the premise that certain concepts and descriptions put forward forty years ago by Guy Debord and the Situationist International, as part of their effort to comprehend the new forms of state control and social disintegration then emerging, still possess explanatory power – more so than ever, we suspect, in the poisonous epoch we are living through. In particular, the twinned notions of "the colonization of everyday life" and "the society of the spectacle" – we think each concept needs the other if either is to do its proper work – strike us as having purchase on key aspects of what has happened since September 11, 2001. Our purpose, in a word, is to turn two central Situationist hypotheses back to the task for which they were always primarily intended – to make them instruments of political analysis again, directed to an understanding of the powers and vulnerabilities of the capitalist state. (We take it we are not alone in shuddering at the way "spectacle" has taken its place in approved postmodern discourse over the past fifteen years – as a vaguely millenarian accompaniment to "new media studies" or to wishful thinking about freedom in cyberspace, with never a whisper that its original objects were the Watts Riots and the Proletarian Cultural Revolution.)

None of this means that we think we comprehend the whole shape and dynamic of the new state of affairs, or can offer a theory of its deepest determinants. We are not sectaries of the spectacle; no one concept, or cluster of concepts, seems to us to get the measure of the horror of the past four years. We even find it understandable, if in the end a mistake, that some on the Left have seen the recent wars in the desert and squabbles in the Security Council as open to analysis in classical Marxist terms, proudly unreconstructed – bringing on stage again the predictions and revulsions of Lenin's and Hobson's studies of imperialism – rather than in those of a politics of "internal", technologized social control.[7]

---

7 This is not meant to signal that we believe that all the key terms of Marx's analysis have outlived their usefulness. Our discussion of "primitive accumulation" has already indicated

This much we are sure of. What is new in the current dark circumstance still largely eludes analysis. Any such analysis is obliged to begin from three obvious, interlinked questions of the moment, which now we set out in tabular form:

- To what extent did the events of September 11, 2001 – the precision bombing of New York and Washington by organized enemies of the US empire – usher in a new era? Did those events change anything fundamental in the calculus and conduct of advanced capitalist states, or in the relation of such states to their civil societies? If so, how?
- Are we to understand the forms of assertion of American power since September 11 – the hasty demonstration of military supremacy (largely to reassure the demonstrators, one feels, that "something could still be done" with the monstrous armory at the state's beck and call), the blundering attempts at recolonization under way in Afghanistan and Iraq, the threats and payoffs to client states in every corner of the globe, the glowering attack on civil liberties within the US itself – as a step backward, *an historical regression*, in which the molecular, integral, invisible means of control which so many of us believed were indispensable to a truly "modern" state-system have given way to a new/old era of gunboats and book-burning?
- Do the concepts "society of the spectacle" and "colonization of everyday life" help us to grasp the logic of the present age? Or has the level of social dispersal and mendaciousness to which those concepts once pointed also been overtaken – displaced, abruptly, at a special moment of urgency and arrogance – by cruder, older imperatives of statecraft?

---

the contrary. It is the "proudly unreconstructed" that is the point at issue here. Too many Marxist commentators lately have struck us as a touch smug (or is it relieved?) in the face of the new imperialism, as if it validated the whole panoply of Marxist explanations, and put all others in the shade.

None of these questions, to repeat, can be answered in isolation. No one level of analysis – "economic" or "political", global or local, focusing on the means of either material or symbolic production – will do justice to the current strange mixture of chaos and grand design. But one main aspect of the story – the struggle for mastery in the realm of the image – has so far been barely thought of as *positively interacting* with others more familiar and "material". It is the first outline of this inter-action we aim to offer, for further debate.

I

The version of "spectacle" with which we operate is minimal, pragmatic, and matter of fact. No doubt the idea's original author often gave it an exultant, world-historical force. But his tone is inimitable, as all efforts to duplicate it have proven; and in any case we are convinced that the age demands a different cadence – something closer (if we are lucky) to that of the lines from *Paradise Lost* we use as our epigraph than to anything from Lukács or Ducasse.

The notion "spectacle" was intended, then, as a first stab at charac-terizing a new form of, or stage in, the accumulation of capital. What it named preeminently was the submission of more and more facets of human sociability – areas of everyday life, forms of recreation, patterns of speech, idioms of local solidarity, kinds of ethical or aesthetic insubordination, the endless capacities of human beings to evade or refuse the orders brought down to them from on high – to the deadly solicitations (the lifeless bright sameness) of the market. Those who developed the analysis in the first place resisted the idea that this colonization of everyday life was dependent on any one set of tech-nologies, but notoriously they were interested in the means modern societies have at their disposal to systematize and disseminate appear-ances, and to subject the texture of day-to-day living to a constant barrage of images, instructions, slogans, logos, false promises, virtual realities, miniature happiness-motifs. Batteries Not Included, as the old punk band had it.

The choice of the word "colonization" to describe the process was deliberate. It invited readers to conceive of the invasion and sterilizing of so many unoccupied areas of human species-being – areas that previous regimes, however overweening, had chosen (or been obliged) to leave alone – *as a specific necessity of capitalist production,* just as much part of its dynamism as expansion to the ends of the earth. The colonization of everyday life, we might put it from our present vantage point, was "globalization" turned inward – mapping and enclosing the hinterland of the social, and carving out from the detail of human inventiveness an ever more ramified and standardized market of exchangeable subjectivities. Naturally the one colonization implied the other: there would have been no Black Atlantic of sugars, alcohols, and opiates without the drive to shape subjectivity into a pattern of small (saleable) addictions.

The point of the analysis, again, was to bring into focus the terms and possibilities of resistance (wars of liberation) against the colonizing forces; this in a situation, the later 1960s, where it was not foolhardy, even if ultimately mistaken, to imagine "reassembling our afflicted Powers" and doing real harm to the enemy. Debord, to speak of him directly, was concerned most of all with the way the subjection of social life to the rule of appearances had led in turn to a distinct form of politics – of state formation and surveillance. His opinion on these matters fluctuated: they were the aspect of the present he most loathed, and which regularly elicited his best tirades and worst paranoia. We extract the following propositions from his pages.

First, that slowly but surely the state in the twentieth century had been dragged into full collaboration in the micromanagement of everyday life. The market's necessity became the state's obsession. (We say that this happened slowly, and in a sense against the state's better judgment, because always there existed a tension between the modern state's constant armored other-directedness – its *raison d'être* as a war machine – and capital's insistence that the state come to its aid in the great work of internal policing and packaging. This tension has again been visible over the past four years. We believe it is one key to the obvious incoherence of the state's recent actions.) Second, this deeper and deeper involvement of the state in the day-to-day instrumentation of consumer obedience meant that increasingly it came to live or die by its investment in, and control of, the field of images – the alternative world conjured up by the new battery of "perpetual emotion machines",[8] of which TV was the dim pioneer and which now beckons the citizen every waking minute. This world of images had long been a structural necessity of a capitalism oriented toward the overproduction of commodities, and therefore the constant manufacture of desire for them; but by the late twentieth century it had given rise to a specific polity.

The modern state, we would argue, has come to need weak citizenship. It depends more and more on maintaining an impoverished and hygienized public realm, in which only the ghosts of an older, more idiosyncratic civil society live on. It has adjusted profoundly to its economic master's requirement for a thinned, unobstructed social texture, made up of loosely attached consumer subjects, each locked in its plastic work-station and nuclearized family of four. Weak citizenship, but for that very reason the object of the state's constant, anxious attention – an unstoppable barrage of idiot fashions and panics and image-motifs, all aimed at sewing the citizen back (unobtrusively, "individually") into a deadly simulacrum of community.

Very often, the first writers to confront this nightmare seemed to despair in the face of it:

---

8 Perry Anderson, *The Origins of Postmodernity*, London 1998, p. 89.

There is no place left where people can discuss the realities which concern them, because they can never lastingly free themselves from the crushing presence of media discourse and of the various forces organized to relay it …. Unanswerable lies have succeeded in eliminating public opinion, which first lost the ability to make itself heard and then very quickly dissolved altogether …. Once one controls the mechanism which operates the only form of social verification to be fully and universally recognized, one can say what one likes …. Spectacular power can similarly deny whatever it wishes to, once, or three times over, and change the subject: knowing full well there is no danger of riposte, in its own space or any other.[9]

Too many times over the past four years these sentences, in their very anger and sorrow at the present form of politics, have echoed in our minds. But ultimately we dissent from their totalizing closure. Living after September 11, we are no longer so sure – and do not believe that spectacular power is sure – that "there is no danger of riposte, in its own space or any other". For better or worse, the precision bombings were such a riposte. And their effect on the spectacular state has been profound: the state's reply to them, we are certain, has exceeded in its crassness and futility the martyr-pilots' wildest dreams. Therefore we turn to another sentence from the same book, which (characteristically) acts as finale to the previous admissions of defeat. "To this list of the triumphs of power we should add, however, one result which has proved negative: once the running of the state involves a permanent and massive shortage of historical knowledge, that state can no longer be led *strategically*."[10] Issued by a devotee of Sun Tzu and Clausewitz, this last verdict is crushing.

9 Guy Debord, *Comments on the Society of the Spectacle*, trans. Malcolm Imrie, London 1998 (first published 1988), pp. 13–19 (order of sentences altered).
10 Ibid., p. 20.

Debord had a robust and straightforward view of the necessity, for individuals and collectives, of learning from the past. (It is not the least of the ways his thinking is classical, as opposed to postmodern.) Of course he knew that the past is a "construction"; but a construction, he believed, made of obdurate and three-dimensional materials, constantly resisting any one frame, and which only the most elaborate machinery of forgetting could make fully tractable to power. His deepest fears as a revolutionary derived from the sense, which grew upon him, that this elaborate machinery might now have been built, and really be turning the world into an eternal present. That was the key to his hatred of the image-life: that what it threatened, ultimately, was the very existence of the complex, created, *two-way* temporality that for him constituted the essence of the human.

Such was the nightmare. But even Debord sometimes took (cold) comfort from the recognition that the state too lived the nightmare, and would suffer the consequences. For it too could no longer learn from the past: it had progressively dismantled the contexts in which truly strategic discussion of its aims and interests – thinking in the long term, admitting the paradoxes and uncertainties of power, recognizing, in a word, "the cunning of reason" – might still be possible.[11] The state was entrapped in its own apparatus of clichés. It had come almost to *believe* in the policy-motifs its think-tanks and disinformation consultancies churned out for it. How Debord would have reveled, over the past months, in the endless double entendres provided by the media, to the effect that Bush and Blair's rush to war in Iraq should be blamed on "faulty intelligence"!

---

11 We are not denying that arenas still exist, most of them deeply secret, in which certain aspects of state interest and policy are plotted over the long term. That is notably true, for obvious reasons, of the state's enabling role in economic affairs. No conspiracy theory of history is needed, now that the relevant documentation (or a small part of it) has been teased from the usual sources, to see how elaborate were the tradeoffs between capital and the state in the planning and instrumentation of the whole neo-liberal push. The problem lies not in the

II

What, then, politically and strategically, took place on September 11, 2001? And how, politically and strategically, has the US state responded to it? Of course, we realize the dangers here. Why should we follow the lead of the spectacle itself in electing this one among many atrocities – raised to the new power of ideology, inevitably, by the idiot device of digitalizing its date – as a world-historical turning point? How much of the real dynamic (and pathology) of American power is conjured away by pinning it thus to a single image-event – in much the same way that American victory in the Cold War was rendered in retrospect magical, unanalyzable, by the mantra "the Fall of the Wall"? There have been moments when we found it easy to sympathize with those of our comrades who, partly in reaction to the flood of cloying, pseudo-apocalyptic verbiage released by September 11 (which shows no sign of abating), go so far as to dismiss the bombings as so many pinpricks, *attentats*, hopeless symbolic gestures on the part of those with no real power to wound.

"Hopeless symbolic gestures". We agree quite strictly with all three words of the diagnosis. (As do the perpetrators, it seems. In them chiliasm is spliced with nihilism, to form a distinctively hyper-modern compound. When they boast in their communiqués of being "for Death" – in contradistinction, they imply, to modernity's miserable attachment to a Life not worth the name – one is never sure if one is hearing Tyndale's cry from the stake or Stavrogin's in the last pages of *The Possessed*. As so often lately, the twenty-first century seems an amalgam of the sixteenth and nineteenth.) And the question remains:

---

state's inability to think *capitalism* strategically – for here real ruthlessness, lucidity, and expertise are at its disposal, and able to insist on their need for policy as opposed to slogans – but on the lack of adequate contexts in which these economic imperatives can be coordinated with others, equally vital to the state's well-being: with "balance of power" geopolitics, notably, and with the changing nature and efficacy of warfare as an instrument of policy, and, above all, with the new valencies of ideological (both "cultural" and first-level "political") struggle.

What is the *effectiveness* – the specific political force – of this form of symbolic action, hopeless or not, within the symbolic economy called "spectacle"? *Spectacularly*, the American state suffered a defeat on September 11. And spectacularly, for this state, does not mean superficially or epiphenomenally. The state was wounded in September in its heart of hearts, and we see it still, almost four years later, flailing blindly in the face of an image it cannot exorcize, and trying desperately to convert the defeat back into terms it can respond to.

One last caveat. Is it necessary to state that because we refuse to extract the September bombings from the cycle of horrors over which the US has presided since 1945, and believe it necessary, if we are to understand them politically, to treat the events of September as an occurrence in a war of images, it does not follow that we fail to recognize (and wish we could find words for) the events' obscenity? We hope not. On the contrary, precisely because the attacks in September were calibrated to leave an indelible image-trail behind them, they have seared in the memory item after item of evidence of just what it is, in terms of human fear and agony, that political calculus so habitually writes off. We too are haunted by the flailing arms of the jumpers, and the scream on the soundtrack as the tower stutters into dust; just as we are haunted by the image of Hanadi Jaradat's bloody head, "her thick hair tied in a ponytail", dumped by the clean-up squad on a table at the back of the restaurant in Haifa she had blown to pieces an hour before.[12] We wish we had words for these things. We wish we lived in a political culture where the language of revulsion had not been debauched by decade after decade of selective gravitas. (Your Chechnya for my Guatemala. Your Suharto for my Pol Pot.)

We proceed then, unwillingly, from the image on the screen. It matters profoundly, we are convinced, that the horrors of September 11 were

---

12 *New York Times*, October 5, 2003.

designed above all to be visible, and that this visibility marked the bombings off from most previous campaigns of air terror, especially those sponsored by states. There were no cameras at Dresden, Hamburg, and Hiroshima.[13] The horror there had to be unseen; it had to act – was meant to act – on the surrounding population in the form of uncontrollable hearsay and panic; and it was to be presented to the enemy state apparatus in the form of report, statistic, prediction, ultimata.

September's terror was different. It made no demands, it offered no explanations. It was premised on the belief (learned from the culture it wishes to annihilate) that a picture is worth a thousand words – that a picture, in the present condition of politics, is itself, if sufficiently well executed, a specific and effective piece of statecraft. Of course the martyr-pilots knew that bringing down the Twin Towers would do nothing, or next to nothing, to stop the actual circuits of capital. But circuits of capital are bound up, in the longer term, with circuits of sociability – patterns of belief and desire, levels of confidence, degrees of identification with the good life of the commodity. And these, said the terrorists, thinking strategically, are aspects of the social imaginary still (always, interminably) being put together by the perpetual emotion machines. Supposing those machines could be captured for a moment, and on them appeared the perfect image of capitalism's negation. Would that not be enough? Enough truly to destabilize the state and society, and produce a sequence of vauntings and paranoias whose long-term political consequences for the capitalist world order would, at the very least, be unpredictable?

---

13   It was not until a year after Hiroshima, in July 1946, that the twin signs of post-war modernity – the mushroom cloud and the two-piece bathing suit – were given form in and around the Bikini "tests". "Eighteen tons of cinematography equipment and more than half the world's supply of motion picture film were on hand to record the Able and Baker explosions" (Jack Niedenthal, *For the Good of Mankind: A History of the People of Bikini and their Islands*, Majuro, MH 2001, p. 3). Interested readers may also wish to consult Michael Light, *100 Suns*, New York 2003.

Or perhaps *entirely* predictable, from a geopolitical standpoint. "You know our demands", said the martyr-pilots (strictly to themselves). "And we know you cannot accede to them …. We know what you will do instead …. We are certain your answer will be military …. We anticipate your idiot leader blurting out the word crusade …. What you will do will vindicate our analysis point by point, humiliation by humiliation, and confirm the world of Islamism in its despairing strength …. And you will do it because there is no answer to our image-victory, yet you (because humiliation is something in which you have no schooling) have to pretend there is one."[14]

The terrorists (to put it only slightly differently) followed the logic of the spectacle to its charnel-house conclusion. If, to trot out Debord's over-famous aphorism again, "the spectacle is capital accumulated to the point where it becomes image",[15] then what more adequate encapsulation of the process could there be but the World Trade Center (with its multiplication of the terminally gigantic by two)? And what other means of defeating it – its social instrumentality, that is, its power over the consuming imagination – than have it be literally obliterated on camera?

We are rehearsing a logic, not endorsing it. But we believe that only by recognizing what was truly "modern" in the martyr-pilots' strategy – truly the opposite of a desperate, powerless, atavistic pinprick; truly the *instigator* of the state's present agony – will the Left be able to move toward argument with the new terrorism's premises and upshots. At the level of the image (here is premise number one) the state is vulnerable; and that level is now fully part of, necessary to, the state's apparatus of

---

14 In an al-Qaida statement released in the wake of the Madrid bombings, the organization announced that it hoped Bush would win the November election, because he acts "with force not wisdom", and "Being targeted by an enemy is what will wake us from our slumber". Cited in M. Rodenbeck, 'Islam Confronts Its Demons', *New York Review of Books*, April 29, 2004, p. 16.

15 Guy Debord, *The Society of the Spectacle*, trans. Donald Nicholson-Smith, New York 1994 (first pub. 1967), p. 24 .

self-reproduction. Terror can take over the image-machinery for a moment – and a moment, in the timeless echo chamber of the spectacle, may now eternally be all there is – and use it to amplify, reiterate, accumulate the sheer visible happening of defeat. It is a confirmation of the terrorists' hopes that after the first days, in the US, the fall of the Towers became exactly the image that *had not to be shown*.[16] The taboo only made the afterimage more palpable and effective. Everything in the culture went on, and still goes on, in relation to that past image-event; nothing in the culture can address the event directly. The silence of so-called "popular culture" in the face of September 11 has been deafening. (It is as if the commercial music of America in the mid-twentieth century had had nothing to say about war, or race, or the Depression, or the new world of goods and appliances. It had plenty – partly because the adjective "popular" still pointed to something real about its audiences and raw materials. That was long ago, of course: the present total obedience of the culture industry to the protocols of the War on Terror – its immediate ingestion and reproduction of the state's interdicts and paranoias – is proof positive, if any were needed, of the snuffing out of the last traces of insubordination in the studios of Time Warner.)

The logic of the pilots was part fantasy, we would argue, part (proven) lucidity. We could reply to it by saying that the new terrorists succumbed to the temptation of the spectacle, rather than devising a way to outflank or contest it. They were exponents of the idea (brilliant exponents, but this only reveals the idea's fundamental heartlessness) that control over the image is now the key to social power; and that image-power, like all other forms of ownership and ascendancy under capitalism, has been subject to an ineluctable process of concentration, so that now it is manifest in certain identifiable (targetable) places,

---

16 A Bush campaign commercial in March 2004 broke the rule of invisibility, and was taken off the air (with grovelling apologies) in a matter of hours.

monuments, pseudo-bodies, icons, logos, manufactured non-events; signs that in their very emptiness and worthlessness (the Twin Towers as architecture were perfect examples) rule the imaginary earth; and whose concentrated, materialized nullity gives the new terror a chance – to frighten, demoralize, turn the world upside down.

Once upon a time (and still, as we write) bombers went out into the city with their sensible holdalls, or their windbreakers a little more tightly zipped than usual. Once upon a time the shrapnel sliced through livers and skulls in neighborhood restaurants, street markets, dance halls, breeding the contagion of rumor in the narrow streets, sapping the will of a class or colonial enemy, driving its cadres back into the isolation – the demoralization – of "home"; eroding, that is, the patterns of sociability (patterns of fear and enforcement, yes, but embedded in a wider and deeper universe of loyalties) that had held a regime together.

Now a new breed of bomber has understood that in the society they are attacking such networks of sociability are secondary: not absent, not irrelevant, but increasingly supplanted by a ghost sociability which does not need its citizens to leave home for its key rituals and allegiances to reproduce themselves. The terror of September 11 had a handful of targets (our tendency to make it, in memory, simply "the bombing of the Twin Towers" is not untrue to the logic of the event). The perpetrators knew full well that they lacked the means to spread out through the wider social fabric and bring day-to-day business to a halt. And they believed, rightly or wrongly, that in present circumstances they did not need to. What they did was designed to hold us indoors, to make us turn back and back to a moving image of capitalism screaming and exploding, to make us go on listening (in spite of ourselves) to the odious talking heads trying to put something, anything, in place of the desolation.

III

More than one commentator since September 11, particularly over the last two years or so, has tried to make sense of the special desperation of the state's conduct in the aftermath. David Runciman has gone so far as to argue that what is happening amounts to a genuine mutation of the international state system:

> Suddenly, the Hobbesian view that states and states alone have the power to operate under conditions of lawfulness is threatened by the knowledge that even the most powerful states are vulnerable to assault from unknown and unpredictable sources. It can now be said that in the international arena "the weakest has the strength to kill the strongest," or they would do, if only they could get their hands on the necessary equipment. This, potentially, changes everything ....
>
> The common view that 11 September 2001 marked the return to a Hobbesian world is therefore entirely wrong. It marked the beginning of a post-Hobbesian age, in which a new kind of insecurity threatens the familiar structures of modern political life. In one sense, of course, this insecurity is not new, because it carries echoes of the natural uncertainties of individual human beings. But it is new for states, which were meant to be invulnerable to such paranoid anxieties. And since they are not designed to deal with this sort of threat, even the most powerful states don't know what to do about it.[17]

This strikes us as capturing something real. There are several things to be said in response.

First, Runciman's argument starts, very reasonably, from the idea that the state's new level of fearfulness is derived from the possible or actual availability of "weapons of mass destruction" to groups sheltering under

17 David Runciman, "A Bear Armed with a Gun", *London Review of Books*, April 3, 2003, p. 5.

the wing of regimes hostile to the new world order, or rich and skillful enough to bargain with such regimes for a share in their military technology. (The fact that such technology was usually, in the first place, eagerly provided by the states now quaking in their boots at the thought of its going astray – that fact ought to be entered into the reckoning, yes, if it can be done without too much repetitive "I told you so".) It is a slight embarrassment to Runciman that the attack which precipitated the change in the order of state relations used weapons that had nothing to do with the disintegrating international arms market. Nothing could be more foolish, of course, than to leap on Runciman's analysis at this point with sectarian glee, brandishing some tin-pot argument to the effect that from now on the real weapons of mass destruction are the media, that the war is a war of simulacra not bullets – that "the Fall of the Twin Towers Did Not Take Place". But we would argue that the present condition of politics does not make sense unless it is approached from a dual perspective – seen as a struggle for crude, material dominance, but also (threaded ever closer into that struggle) as a battle for the control of appearances.

We agree with Runciman (against many on the Left who would prefer al-Qaida to be a last-gasp, exotic, pathetic, pre-capitalist phenomenon) that the September bombings are a distinctively modern symptom. What they point to, far beyond the specific atrocity and its grisly religious fuel, is a new structural feature of the international state system: that *the historical monopoly of the means of destruction by the state is now at risk*. That new feature has many causes. Technological advance is one of them. The rise of a worldwide secondary market in arms – partly the result of the chaos attending the end of the Cold War, partly a natural product of the neo-liberal commodification of the globe – is another. Likewise the contracting-out of more and more military services to a shady corporate world, again something that neo-liberalism began by warmly recommending to its client nations. The permeability of borders obviously matters, and has become another major item in the new paranoia. But that fact is linked to a deeper and more pervasive reality, which again is a product of the "globalization" these same states are committed to – and on which their bloated home economies depend. *Failed states* is the term of art for this reality – this constitutive feature of the world we live in – from which the personnel and ideology of September 11 so unmistakably arose.

"Failed states", "rogue states", "weak states", "societies left behind by modernization" – the diagnoses are legion, and the facts they point to complex. Let us simply assert here, with the problem of September specifically our object, that "failed states" seem to us a structural element of the international system – a product, a necessity, of the new universe of globalization. There is no ontological distinction between the success-fully weakened and permeable states on which the world order now thrives and those whose weakness has become chronic fatigue and disintegration, and whose embrace of foreign capital has widened just enough to include independent arms dealers, warlords, and drug cartels.

There is a link here, clearly, to our previous argument about the necessity of weak citizenship to the state's internal health. *Weak citizenship*, then, at the spectacular center; and *weak states* in the "world economy" which the center works endlessly to exploit. A weak state is one whose local defenses against imperial control have (through the implanting of "bases", the rifling of natural resources, the helping hand to local elites in the event of indigenous revolt, and neo-liberal penetration by the corporations) all been satisfactorily dismantled. A failed state is one where the logic of abjection has been carried, often imperceptibly, too far – so that suddenly the "flourishing" economy shatters, the bribes no longer produce the shoddy goods, the death rates climb, the effigies of Uncle Sam are paraded through the streets, and up in the mountains or in the university dormitories young men and women cover their heads and study *The Art of War*. We could say with only the slightest edge of exaggeration that failed states are the typical – determinant – political entities of the world left behind by the Cold War, "crash programs", and the attentions of the IMF.

The events of September, it is common knowledge, were directly the creature of this world of despair. They were trained for in Jalalabad, paid for in Riyadh. But saying so does not in the least conflict with the perspective – that of spectacle – from which this chapter began. One of the key phenomena of the "failed state" reality we have been describing is the power of al-Jazeera, and the runaway world of Islamist websites (as the US has learned, much to its chagrin.) Nothing enrages a certain young Arab intellectual so much as the sight of people his own age, surrounded by an urban fabric arrested midway on the path to post-modern squalor, clutching their cellphones and telling their video worry beads. One of the formative moments in the education of Muhammad Atta, we are told, was when he came to realize that the "conservation" of Islamic Cairo, in which he had hoped to participate as a newly trained town planner, was to obey the logic of Disney World.

Failed states are a hideous amalgam of the feudal, the Nasserite "national", *and* the spectacular – that is the point. Intellectuals brought up in such circles of hell need no lessons from postmodern theory about where power lies in the chaos around them, and what means might be available to contest it. They draw conclusions – cruel and mistaken ones, in our view, but emerging from a treadmill of pain and hopelessness we can only dimly guess at – and choose their weapons.

V

We return to the pivotal sentence from Debord. "To this list of the triumphs of power we should add one result which has proved negative: once the running of the state involves a permanent and massive shortage of historical knowledge, that state can no longer be led *strategically*." This can be unpacked in various ways. First, there is what we might call the

Kissinger problem – the problem of weak citizenship in relation to the actual, brutal needs of empire. (This is understandably an obsession of the old Peace-Prizeman. He for one has never recovered from the Vietnam syndrome.) A tension exists – let us put it mildly – between the dispersal and vacuity of the public sphere, which is necessary to the main-tenance of "consumer society", and those stronger allegiances and identifications which the state must call on, repeatedly, if it is to maintain the dependencies that feed the consumer beast. Weak citizens grow too soon tired of wars and occupations. To this long-term dilemma is now added another. A state that lives more and more in and through a regime of the image does not know what to do when, for a moment, it dies by the same lights. It does not matter, as we have said before, that "econom-ically" or "geopolitically" the death may be an illusion. Spectacularly it was real. And image-death – image-defeat – is not a condition this state can endure. "There now exists a threat", to quote Runciman, "which makes some states feel more vulnerable than their subjects."

We would put it differently. Of course, as materialists, *we do not believe that one can destroy the society of the spectacle by producing the spectacle of its destruction.* This is the nub of our tactical dissent from September 11, leaving aside our strategic rejection of terror as a political means (of which more later). But the present state does not share our skepticism, it seems. It feels the cold hand of the image-event at its throat. It lives and relives the moment its machines always had lying in wait for it – the violent rendezvous of speed with enormity, the non-human of technology meeting the non-human of accumulation. As if Cheops himself had looked on while the Great Pyramid was split in two by a bolt from the sun. Just in time for *Good Morning America.*

The spectacular state is obliged, we are saying, to devise an answer to the defeat of September 11. And it seems it cannot. Of course many of the things it has tried out over the past four years have ordinary military, neo-colonial, grossly economic logics underlying them. The invasion of

Iraq is the obvious case in point. We too take seriously the idea that factions within the US administration had long thought the impasse of "sanctions" intolerable, had thirsted for oil, had dreamt of a new bridge-head in an increasingly anti-American region, and so on. These arguments we shall return to. But at the very least it can be said that the manner in which these policies were acted on finally – they had been the pipe dreams of the ultra-Right in Washington for more than a decade – has been a barely credible mixture of blunder, gullibility, overreach, lip-smacking callousness (hardly bothering to disguise its lack of concern at the "stuff happening" in the streets of Kandahar or Baghdad), unfath-omable ignorance and wishful thinking, and constant entrapment in the day-to-day, hour-by-hour temporality of the sound bite and the suicide bomb. And where, in the end, is the image the war machine has been looking for – the one to put paid to the September haunting? Toppling statues, Presidents in flight jackets, Saddam saying "Aah", embedded toadies stroking the barrels of guns … wake us (wake the whole world of couch potatoes) when it's over.

The Towers keep falling; and now they are joined by the imagery of Abu Ghraib. One studiously moderate historian of the age of European empire had this to say, recently, about what marked the colonized world off from the generality of empires preceding it.

Europeans were by no means the only rulers with a superiority complex *vis-à-vis* their subjects. But they displayed this complex in an exceptionally systematic, self-conscious way, and in an unusually wide range of symbolic settings. They were ingenious in devising methods to humiliate non-Europeans, and unusually skilled at encouraging those they ruled to internalize an inferiority complex.[18]

18 David Abernethy, *The Dynamics of Global Dominance: European Overseas Empires 1415–1980*, New Haven and London 2000, p. 12.

"An unusually wide range of symbolic settings." Of course the setting
in the photograph we use as our frontispiece is in a sense ordinary,
unimaginative. The box, the hood, the wires, the electrodes – these are
the banalities of evil. The US is still learning the ropes. What is extraordinary, nonetheless, is the fact of torture and dehumanization becoming
an *image* in the way they did here – in the midst of a battle for "hearts
and minds" – and one that instantly dismantled the rhetoric of liberation. It did so because it concentrated – crystallized – a whole previous
history of horror and resistance. "Traffic was flowing freely again
through the city's eastern gateway at the Square of the 1920
Revolution", reported the *New York Times* during a lull in the battle for
Najaf. And added by way of explanation: "a monument to a Shi'ite
uprising against British troops".[19] (It might have explained further: an
uprising that took place just two years after Britain created the entity
called Iraq, taking the colonizers utterly by surprise.) Thus the export of
democracy continues.

V

It seems that the state does not know what to do in these circumstances.
This does not mean it is on the path to real strategic failure, necessarily,
or that it will prove incapable of pulling back from the imperatives of
the image-war and slowly, relentlessly, accommodating itself to the needs
of a new round of primitive accumulation. The hatchet men and torture
brigades (professionals, not part-timers from Appalachia) are being
retrained as we write. "Road maps" are to be thrown in the trash can.
Failed states become weak states once more. "Democracy" proves unex-
portable. Iran and Syria join the comity of nations. Exit Wolfowitz and
Makiya, mumbling.

19 *New York Times*, August 14, 2004.

States can behave like maddened beasts, in other words, and still get their way. They regularly do. But the present madness is singular: the dimension of spectacle has never before interfered so palpably, so insistently, with the business of keeping one's satrapies in order. And never before have spectacular politics been conducted in the shadow – the "historical knowledge" – of *defeat*. It remains to be seen what new mutation of the military-industrial-entertainment complex emerges from the shambles.

2

BLOOD FOR OIL?

[Oil] is a filthy, foul smelling liquid that squirts obligingly up into the air and falls back to earth as a rustling shower of money.

—Ryszard Kapuscinski, *The Shah of Shahs*

Capitalism presents itself, said Marx on more than one occasion, as an "immense accumulation of commodities". The commodity is the economic cell-form of capital – its basic genetic material. Oil, a perfect specimen of the cell-form, derives its power from a double identity, a twofold belonging to the human world. On the one hand – and what could be simpler? – a commodity offers itself as an object for use, an "expedient thing" whose semantics can be traced back to early modern notions of income and profit. But on the other, in a full-scale commodity-producing economy, what comes to matter about each separate article is not so much its constellation of uses as its value as an item of exchange, the commodity's function as a "material depository" (the language is taken from Marx once again) of exchange value.

The exact relation between the depository and its value turns out to be somewhat obscure, but value seems to be generated from the commodity's shifting place in a complex, self-contained world of money equivalents. So that finally the foul-smelling liquidity (and combustibility) of petroleum presents itself as merely the outward and accidental appearance of something more basic, more primary: the article's price. The rustling shower of money becomes what "oil" truly is.

Yet oil's price, and the forces that surround its determination, remain mysterious, confusing. Because petroleum and basic resources in general are part of a bewildering world of appearances that veil the operations of the economy. It is no accident that Marx ends his account of commodities in *Capital* not with the intricacies of value or the acrobatics of price determination as such, but with the difficulty of seeing through the commodity form; of coming to terms with the talismanic qualities of commodities – their "metaphysical subtleties" and "theological niceties" – that occlude their true character. The commodity is always something other than what it seems.

In the long march toward the modern world system, *mass* commodities – gold, sugar, slaves, cotton, coal, oil – have been its beasts of burden. They have sometimes served as markers for entire historical epochs. If such commodities bear the mark (now, mostly disguised) of capitalism's original sin – "dripping from head to foot ... with blood and dirt", as Marx put it, characteristically – they each also come to be invested with their own specific mythos, their own magic power: King Cotton, Black Gold, Silicon Valley. Capitalism would be nothing without its continual ability to make materials (or men and women reduced to the status of materials) the Creators of New Worlds. For all the talk lately about the emergence of a post-industrial economy – in which "information" or "services" or "symbol-management" is already, we are told, displacing the authority of any one material resource – the last few years have been an object lesson in just how vital to this dream of the future remains the control of a few strategic commodities. Blood and dirt cling to them still. They are the motors of production, the ultimate hard currency of exchange. But *for that very reason* they are subject to the deepest and most complete mystification.

Never more so than in the case of oil. The great Polish journalist

Ryszard Kapuscinksi, living through the spectacular oil boom of the 1970s in West Asia, fully sensed the mysteries of Black Gold:

> [O]il creates the illusion of a completely changed life, life without work, life for free, it expresses the eternal human dream of wealth achieved through a lucky accident … in this sense it is a fairy tale, and like all fairy tales a bit of a lie.[20]

Commentators on the present ills of the world contribute to oil's mystification: oil is a "curse", they say, it "distorts" the natural course of development and ushers in an economy of hyper-consumption and excess: golf courses in the Saudi desert, bloated shopping malls – stacked with the detritus of trans-Atlantic capitalism – in Dubai and Bahrain. Democracy is "hindered" by oil (as if cobalt promoted constitutional government), installing despotic rule and patrimonialism rather than statecraft and capitalist discipline. There is ring of truth here. But it is thin and shallow because it substitutes a brand of narrow commodity determinism for the larger truths of primitive accumulation – the deadly complicity, that is to say, of guns, oil, and money.

At various points in this book we gesture back to the street demonstrations of February and March 2003; sometimes in awe at the moment's vitality and momentum, sometimes in frustration at its limits. If there was a single political thread tying the anti-war mobilizations together, it was undoubtedly the refrain of "No Blood for Oil". A flotilla of signs rang variants on the idea, and on Market Street in San Francisco it was Chevron headquarters (not Bechtel or Carlyle or Starbucks) that goaded the marchers to their most vocal dissent.

---

20 *The Shah of Shahs,* New York 1982, p. 36.

And with good reason. The American addiction to cheap petroleum had shepherded the brokers, carpetbaggers, and hustlers of the oil business directly into political office. Five "supermajors" – elephantine oil corporations with wells, pipelines, refineries, and subsidiaries in almost every country on earth, more gluttonous and powerful than ever after the great round of mergers during the 1990s[21] – had scaled the walls of the White House. The more flagrant and vulgar the identity of interests the better. In a bullish five years as CEO of the world's largest oil-and-gas-services company, Vice President Cheney had siphoned $44 million in salary from Halliburton – heading an outfit that on his own Brechtian admission saw war as a "growth opportunity". Millions more dollars in "deferred compensation" were earmarked to tide him over during his time away from the trough. As if to signal that Cheney's view of politics now ruled unopposed in Washington, in December 2003 the administration trotted out the Bush family *consigliere*, James Baker – the consummate oil man – as Special Presidential Envoy to restructure Iraq's $130 billion debt.[22] Baker's mission, we now know, was less about debt-forgiveness than cutting a deal for the Carlyle Group (for whom Baker is senior counselor). Carlyle was to receive a $1 billion investment from Kuwait as a quid pro quo for restructuring Iraq's liabilities, thereby guaranteeing Kuwait – and various oil companies – billions of dollars in war reparations, still due from Iraq as a result of the First Gulf War. Good business if you can get it.

A sector of American capital, in other words – and a commodity whose geo-strategic significance had obsessed the American establishment

---

21 Exxon-Mobil, Royal Dutch-Shell, BP-Amoco, TotalFinaElf, and Chevron-Texaco have collective sales revenues of over $500 billion (almost twice the GDP of all of sub-Saharan Africa).

22 Baker's law firm represents Halliburton; Baker Hughes, his oil-services company, was promised the restoration of second-tier oil fields after Kellogg, Brown and Root; and he is a member of the ruling politburo of the Carlyle Group, in which it is estimated he owns equity to the value of $180 million – a sliver of their $17.5 billion portfolio.

ever since World War Two – had finally achieved transcendent power. How could it be doubted that the war against Saddam was to be fought essentially for possession of petroleum, and that the subsequent occupation would aim at giving the US permanent control of a crucial spigot?

How could it be doubted? If the last four years are not a compelling confirmation of economic determinism in the last instance – the economic base deciding the political superstructure – then what ever will be? We take the point of these rhetorical questions, but shall proceed in what follows to question the entire logical structure of the Blood for Oil argument. We distrust its false transparency. We think it *aspires* to be an economic explanation of history, but is really still locked inside a "hero-and-villains" vision of social process. It revolves around the (malign) power of a single commodity, substituting the facticity of oil (and oil men) for the complex, partially *non*-factual imperatives of capital accumulation.

Let us set out our ambitions for this chapter as unambiguously as we can. We shall pursue four lines of inquiry. The first aims to identify the broad contours of the Blood for Oil account – in the process putting the thesis itself in the strongest form we can manage. The second goes on to expose the actual complexity, and the heterogeneous form, of the oil argument when it is deployed as anything more than a slogan (and in so doing we hope to demonstrate that the argument itself, pursued at all seriously, compels its users to move beyond oil as such). We then provide our own reading of oil politics; namely, a synoptic view of the constitutive role of oil in American empire, but one that exposes, and questions, Blood for Oil's Malthusian underpinning – its presumption that the control of oil led ineluctably to war, and most of all, its unwillingness to situate oil on the larger landscape of capital. Finally, we turn to the occupation of Iraq, and try to situate American policy in the Middle East in relation to the full spectrum of capital's needs and appetites over the past decade. Here we address the question of primitive accumulation, but try above all to rethink that recurrent (and ancient) form of capitalist expansion in relation to the present-day configuration of US power worldwide – the *military neo-liberalism* which characterizes American empire in its twenty-first century iteration. The invasion and occupation of Iraq must ultimately be located, in our view, in the deadly alchemy of permanent war, capitalist accumulation, and the new enclosures – all now conducted under conditions of the spectacle.

What follows is sometimes technical, not to say tortuous. We see no way out of this. Capitalism is technical, and certainly tortuous. It is not necessary for the Left always to follow its convolutions – we think the Left has regularly suffered from an infatuation with its enemy's mechanics – but sometimes it is. The Blood for Oil argument claims to provide an account of capitalist politics. We believe it does not. Our obligation to the reader, therefore, is to establish what a genuine account would consist of.

I

What is the logical structure of the Blood for Oil thesis? The US attacked Iraq, wrote George Monbiot in the *Guardian*, because "Iraq had something it wanted".[23] Something scarce, finite, exhaustible – and indispensable. No effort was made to disguise the war's basic purpose: from the very beginning, Bush had been "making plans for the day when oil production peaks, by seeking to secure the reserves of other nations". In capsule form, Monbiot identified the three basic assertions of the blood-oil couplet: *strategic use* ("without oil most Americans could not get to work"), *Malthusian scarcity* (the "peaking" of world production), and *geopolitics* (the strange political geography of oil reserves). War for oil was

---

23 George Monbiot, "Bottom of the Barrel", *Guardian*, December 2, 2003.

premeditated and tied to one central imperative. The White House now acted as the executive committee of the American Petroleum Institute.

Almost invariably, this line of argument turns on a plotting – a mapping – of personal connections, Big Oil business networks, and the revolving door of government-corporate power: the kindred Houses of Bush and Saud; the Carlyle Group and its ties to bin Laden family assets; Prince Bandar's Washington influence; Manchurian Global; no-bid contracts; and so on. Stepping back from the detail of conspiracy theory (as we have said before, never was a conspiracy less interested in concealment), Cheney's April 2001 *National Energy Strategy*, crafted early in the Bush presidency by oil lobbyists and executives, is often held to provide the state's own explicit set of justifications – of predictions, even – concerning the blood for oil linkage. US oil consumption (over a quarter of global output) is estimated to rise by over 30 percent by 2020; and no more than a quarter of that increase, the report reckoned, was likely to come from a new round of domestic production. The ruin of Alaska would hardly make a dent in the problem. More ominously, the contribution of the Middle East to global oil output was projected to grow from 25 percent to 40 percent. The SUV economy (by now we are paraphrasing Cheney's report a touch freely) had paved the way for "increased dependency on foreign powers that do not always have America's interests at heart."

In the dizzying world of oil addiction,[24] Iraq had displaced Saudi Arabia as a "swing producer"[25] – "turning its taps on and off when … it was in its strategic interest". And Saddam's destabilizing influence

---

24 The statistics bear repeating. In 2000, the US consumed over 1100 gallons of petrol per capita; the other OECD countries averaged roughly 400 gallons per person. The remainder of the planet used less than one tenth of the US figure.

25 Saudi Arabia is a member of OPEC, but it is a measure of the bizarre world of global oil politics that the US government has, in its "special relationship" with the House of Saud, expected the Saudis to maintain sufficient unused capacity to compensate for any short term market tightening or price volatility. It was Saudi Arabia that released oil to stall the OPEC price rises in 1973 and during the 1990–91 Gulf War. Within twenty-four hours of September 11, 9 million extra barrels of Saudi oil were released to keep prices stable.

("a demonstrated willingness to use the oil weapon") raised the possibility of a future "need for military intervention".[26] There was even a
1975 feasibility study – prepared by the Congressional Research Service
for the House Subcommittee on International Relations – that could be
dusted off for specific advice on "Oilfields as Military Objectives".

Why did Iraq figure so prominently in the *National Energy Strategy*'s
calculations? A number of developments – political turbulence within
the House of Saud, centering on the succession of King Fahd; insurgent Wahhabism in the kingdom (with a direct line to the September 11
attacks); signs of a Saudi–Iranian rapprochement; a new assertiveness
by other OPEC powers; and the dismal findings of the Simmons
Report,[27] spelling out the declining present and future yields of major
Saudi oil fields – had conspired to place in doubt the Saudi role as reliable swing producer. The other pillar of post-war US oil policy – Iran
– was long lost to revolutionary Islam. Now Saudi Arabia had become
a dangerous mess. According to the *Arab Human Development Report*, the
kingdom ranked last in the region on all key indicators of "democracy"
and "social achievement". No mean feat, given the competition. Per
capita income in 1981 had been $28,000 a year; by 2002 it had plum-
meted to $8,000. The population had quadrupled since 1970: a quarter
of a million young men enter the inhospitable labor market each year.
Actual conditions cannot be determined with any precision ("we don't
have a tradition of statistics" says a Saudi banker); officially, unemployment is around 10 percent, but it may be as much as three or four times

26 In a top-secret National Security Council document, NSC staff were directed to cooperate
    fully with Cheney's Energy Task Force as its core mission included the "melding" of two
    policy arenas: "the review of operational policies toward rogue states" and "actions regarding
    the capture of new and existing oil fields".
27 Matthew Simmons, investment bank president, is an advisor to Cheney. His report docu-
    mented the degraded condition of Saudi oil fields (due in part to massive pumping of
    seawater to facilitate extraction). Simmons estimated a rate of decline of 8 percent for the
    major Ghawar field and emphasized the need to bring older fields back into production
    (*New York Times*, February 24, 2004).

that figure among the young. More than half the high school curriculum consists of religious instruction, and half the country's youth say they are planning to emigrate. The country has no secular charities, no non-religious NGOs, and no political parties. If free elections were held tomorrow in Saudi Arabia, so one Western European ambassador had it, bin Laden would win hands down.

Iraq, by contrast, was awash with low-cost oil. As yet only 15 of its 74 fields have been developed; known reserves are 112 billion barrels, but once the new technologies for subsurface exploration become operational, Iraqi holdings might exceed 300 billion barrels (perhaps one quarter of global reserves) over the coming decade. What made Iraq special, said Paul Wolfowitz to the APEC powers in Singapore, was that it "floats on a sea of oil". With recovery rates of 50 percent (a conservative figure) and reserves of 250 billion barrels (an equally cautious reckoning), Iraqi oil would be worth about $3.125 trillion. To this can be added the bonus of 100 trillion cubic feet of natural gas – sufficient to supply the entire US for ten years or more. Not to mention the fact that compromised fields in Kirkuk and Rumaila, plus the sanctions-era degradation of basic oil infrastructure (more than $60 billion of needed repairs, the industry estimated), held out the promise of bottomless state contracts for the likes of Bechtel, and Kellogg, Brown and Root – the "next Klondike" as the US Overseas Private Investment Corporation delicately put it.[28] Providing, of course, that a pliant and stable Iraq could be installed to administer the no-bidding.

Shock and awe offered the prospect, as Thomas Friedman said at the time, of killing two birds with one stone: "Destroy Saddam and destabilize OPEC".[29] Or, more precisely, the war promised a return to the good *old* days of OPEC – oil prices kept low enough to lubricate American

28 In 2003 alone, Halliburton's Iraq contracts represented 22.1 percent of its total revenues.
29 Thomas Friedman, "Oil price formula calls for critical maths if Saddam is taken out of the equation", *Guardian*, August 6, 2002, p. 6.

capitalism and satisfy the US consumer, but high enough to feed oil company profits; oil quotas sufficient to line the pockets of supplicant petro-oligarchies around the world; a marker price within a zone capable of drawing non-OPEC oil into the world market as a buffer; and, once again, an obedient swing producer willing and able to respond to the exigencies and volatilities ("supply-disruption risk", in the argot of the New York Mercantile Exchange) of the earth's most strategic commodity. Had not the 2001 Baker Institute Report (yes, *that* Baker), *Strategic Energy Policy Challenges for the 21st Century*, noted the disturbing rundown in spare capacity worldwide? (OPEC's unused sources of supply had amounted to 25 percent of global demand in 1985; by 1990 they made up no more than 2 percent.) The earth, it concluded, was "precariously close to utilizing all of its available global oil production", thereby "raising the chances of an oil supply crisis". The occupation of Iraq promised a resolution to all this. And more.

An oil war offered the rosy prospect of "privatization by occupation" – or, a "sublime" opportunity to "scoop up cheap assets" as STRATFOR put it.[30] Whether or not existing French and Russian contracts with the Ba'athist state would be honored was of less consequence to the oil supermajors than the prospect of a neo-liberal assault, led by Rumsfeld and Cheney, on Iraq's nationalized oil industry, a staple of all Third World petro-states and a sector that had in general escaped the fate of neo-liberal privatization. And behind this hostility to state-owned petroleum lay a bitter, and complex, history. The patchwork of foreign concessions and informal state-company alliances that had dominated the first part of the twentieth century – the so-called era of "free-flowing oil" – had been ripped apart by insurgent nationalisms during the post-1945 period, with Venezuela and Iran leading the charge. US oil companies had turned, not

---

30 Strategic Forecasting Inc., the self-described "world's leading private intelligence provider" based in Texas (www.stratfor.com), quoted in C. Brightman, *Total Insecurity*, London 2004, p. 215.

unexpectedly, to the US state for support: they were duly provided with foreign tax credits to compensate for rising royalty payments in the world at large, with tariffs on the importation of cheap overseas oil, with exemptions from anti-trust prosecution, and, most dramatically, with a CIA-backed coup to topple the Mosadeq government in Iran. But all this, in a sense, proved futile. The new geography of oil cartels, and the founding of OPEC in 1960, marked an historic politicization – and ultimately the global restructuring – of the oil business.

Of course, none of this meant the collapse of profitability for the likes of Shell and Amoco. Quite the reverse: the new "limited flow" arrangement was predicated, as Sheik Yamani put it, on not wanting "the majors to lose their power". (For every dollar increase in the price of crude during the 1970s, the majors increased their net profits by 7 percent.) Nevertheless, the Seven Sisters were compelled to live with a new international oil system, accepting "upstream" nationalization and an effective Third World cartel as (unpleasant) facts of life. In response, the majors moved "downstream" in many key activities, operating as joint ventures with national oil firms to whom higher royalties were now paid (the so-called 50/50 system), and consolidating their power in other sectors of the supply chain to compensate for the loss of direct control of reserves. Between 1953 and 1972 their share of concession areas fell from 64 percent to 24 percent. Even after the mergers of the late 1990s, the supermajors directly produced only 35 percent of their sales, and controlled only 4 percent of world reserves.

On this larger canvas, then, Iraq was to be made an example – it would set the stage for a whole new attempt at the radical de-nationalization of oil (a process begun, to little effect, in Saudi Arabia in 1998). By creating an "emerging market" from a decrepit state-owned petroleum industry, the war would lay the foundations for something dear to the hearts of the Washington cabal: an end to (other people's) economic nationalism and producer cartels. Augmented Iraqi output under corporate auspices brought another benefit: OPEC oil would continue to be traded in dollars. (In November 2000 Saddam had switched to the euro as a riposte to Washington's hard line on sanctions.) In this ideological universe, oil figured centrally – since oil had remained one of the Third World's most effective bulwarks against the neo-liberal attack. The appointment of ex-Shell executive Philip Carroll to run the Baghdad energy ministry was a logical move given Paul Bremer's belief (voiced to anyone who would listen) that the Iraqi Governing Council's attachment to oil nationalization "had to be changed". Bremer's first act as proconsul, after all, had been directed at the 190 state-owned companies and their 650,000 employees. He fired half a million of them. What followed was not simply a state liquidation sale but a raft of laws – Order 37 lowering corporate tax rates, Order 39 permitting wholly owned foreign subsidiaries, Order 40 welcoming foreign banks – even more radical than East European shock therapy ("getting Iraq ready for Wal-Mart" as the former Bush–Cheney campaign manager put it).[31] Here was an unprecedented opportunity for BP, Shell, and Exxon-Mobil to take back their old Iraq Petroleum Company possessions. Not just de-nationalization but restitution!

The occupation, everyone agrees, has not gone as planned. Doling out the spoils of war amidst the chaos of a radical insurgency has turned out to be almost impossible – of 2,390 planned projects between 2004 and 2008, only 164 are underway. But who is to say that Bremer and Exxon are not slowly but surely getting what they came for? As always, at taxpayers' expense. Twenty percent of all congressional aid to Iraq has been devoted to oil infrastructure – in effect, a $1.6 billion subsidy to the oil industry. As if to drive home the point, on May 22, 2003 the Bush administration tried to accelerate corporate investment in the Iraqi oil sector by means of Executive Order 13303. A secret order, naturally. It granted non-Iraqi companies blanket immunity from criminal or civil prosecution in relation

---

31 Notably, all of Saddam's laws concerning labor's (lack of) rights were left intact.

to any action – however corrupt, illegal, abusive, or costly to the environ-ment – undertaken with a view to oil exploration, production, or sale.

Such efforts were born partly of desperation. Iraqi oil is at present still flowing (we write in fall 2004), but at a dribble – already in 2003, sabotage had reduced output to 1.33 million barrels per day (bpd), down from 2.12 million bpd the previous year. The occupying armies are incapable of maintaining security in and around the refineries and pipelines. And the extent of the oil infrastructure's ruin has now become clear. One hears much less talk now of that oil-financed imperialism – 7 or 8 million barrels per day was once a common estimate – which not so long ago was the darling of the military accountants. In Rumsfeld-speak: "stuff happens".

There are caveats, then. But even taking account of the present difficulties, does not the story we have told so far add up to a solid confirmation of the Blood for Oil argument? Have not the past two years been both a "bonanza for the American oil companies" (*Washington Post*, September 15, 2002) and "one of the most audacious hostile takeovers ever" (*Wall Street Journal*, April 30, 2003)? Who on the Left would care to disagree?

II

So much for the prosecution case. What are we to make of it? Pitched at a certain level of generality – big actors, deathless economic necessi-ties, corrupt intermediaries, a conception of "capital" as essentially a unified field – the pattern of cause and effect here looks robust. But the argument, under closer scrutiny, turns out to be rather more complex and unstable. The thesis is multilayered, sometimes contradictory, and overconfident that it has put its finger on specific signs of oil at work. In our tally, the Blood for Oil argument might mean that war was launched for any (or all) of the following reasons, or through some concatenation of them:

- Because of an oil shortage (or unacceptably high oil prices), and/or the press of Hubbert's Peak[32] (the zenith of global oil output having been reached).
- Because of the unprecedented powers of the petro-industrial complex (it had captured the White House, as never before).
- Because a self-consciously assertive "oil administration", aware of the need there would be to rehabilitate the vast Iraqi oil sector if ever Saddam was removed from power, could not resist the opportunity for their cronies to drink deep at the well of reconstruction (over 2,300 such projects to be put out to bid for completion over the two years from March 2004).
- Because of a temporary (but strategic) capacity shortage within OPEC.
- Because of a strategic need to reassign Russian and French contracts in Iraq (worth an estimated 70 billion barrels) to the US supermajors.
- Because the privatization of a powerful (and paradigmatic) Third World nationalized oil sector would send a neo-liberal blast through OPEC (indeed, removing Saddam did away with one of OPEC's most assertive voices for aggressive price policy, and set the stage for clipping the wings of another, Hugo Chavez).
- Because of a short-term strategic need to deploy vast oil reserves for geo-strategic purposes. (China's oil consumption is reckoned to be around 10 million bpd by 2020. What a prize, to have gained de facto control over China's industrial progress, as well as leverage over other great oil importers like Germany and Japan!)
- Because the privatization of the Iraqi fields would place pressure on the House of Saud to further deepen the trend, tentatively opened in 1998, to liberalize the Saudi oil sector.

---

32 King Hubbert, a hard-rock geologist, correctly anticipated the peaking of US production in the 1950s, and predicted – less successfully – that world oil output would peak in the year 2000.

- Because war was consistent with the "open-door policy" pursued for the better part of eighty years by the US in the Middle East (and by implication fell in with a "master plan" or "global acquisition strategy"[33] for American control of the great lubricant of hydrocarbon capitalism).
- Because war represented, as in other energy conflicts, a means to restore flagging corporate profitability, low oil prices, and general good order within the oil system worldwide.
- Because of a desire to create a new (and more reliable) "swing producer", friendly to US interests, and thereby maintain the viability of the dollar through petro-dollar based trade.
- Because the whole post-1945 US oil strategy was actually in a shambles (Colombia, Saudi Arabia, Iraq, Nigeria, Indonesia all demonstrably failed states); and in particular, because the capture of Iraqi oil would release the US from the Saudi connection. A collateral benefit of this strategy would be the removal of US troops from the neighborhood of Islam's holiest sites.

This breviary is not exhaustive. Neither is it meant to call in question every one of the claims listed – many have merit, as we shall see. Nonetheless, in our view the Blood for Oil thesis loses sight of what oil ultimately stands for in the present moment: that is, *neo-liberalism mutating from an epoch of "agreements" and austerity programs to one of outright war; the plural and unstable relations among specific forms of capital, always under the banner of some apparently dominant mass commodity; and those periodic waves of capitalist restructuring we call primitive accumulation.* However the argument is unpacked, Blood for Oil misdescribes what a single commodity – despite oil's unique political weight and density – can actually represent in relation to the larger structural imperatives of the system.

33 Mike Davis, "The View from Hubbert's Peak", *Los Angeles Times*, May 26, 2004; Michael Klare, *Resource Wars*, New York 2001.

Kingdom Towers, Riyadh, Saudi Arabia, 2001

This is not quite the same thing as saying that the Blood for Oil argument is crudely reductive – substituting a single motive for a confused, overdetermined set of reasons and causes. At one level this is true. There are almost too many other plausible ways of framing the Iraq invasion: as an exemplary instance of gunboat diplomacy in the interests of "free trade"; as a consequence of the seizure of power by the Project for the New American Century; as a demonstration of the price to be paid by any state opposing the vision of world order laid out in the National Security Strategy document of September 2002; as a road test for Rumsfeld's new model of the military; to permit the withdrawal of US troops from Saudi Arabia; to complete Bush Senior's unfinished business; as a spectacular response to September 11; even as a reaction to the lack of targets in Afghanistan ("we're down to the last outhouse", as Rumsfeld confessed to the *Wall Street Journal*). Whatever the strength of the individual arguments here, together they surely outrun the logic of oil alone.

But this on its own is a feeble objection. All (or most) human situations are overdetermined: it does not follow that the best we can do is settle for a plurality of causes, or a resigned plea for complexity. Some determinants are more important than others; they may shape the logic and limits of the rest. And oil may be such a determinant. The problem with the Blood for Oil hypothesis is not its choice of oil as a dominant factor within a nexus of political economic forces. Rather it has conspicuously failed to grasp the most fundamental properties of imperial oil, and is unable therefore to talk concretely about how oil's dominance is established. Oil's powers are drawn from a quite specific force field having a capitalist core that must periodically reconstitute the conditions of its own profitability.

III

How, then, do *we* position oil, and the global reach of the supermajors, in our interpretation of the Iraq invasion? We begin with two incontestable realities. The first is the brutality of the historical record. Right from the start, commercial oil extraction has been accompanied by ruthless and undisguised imperial violence, by repeated warfare and genocide, and by a cynical lawlessness characteristic of the corporate frontier. Iraq is the result (the deposit) of precisely these processes. The Iraq Petroleum Company (IPC) – reconstituted in 1928 as a consortium made up of the Anglo-Persian Oil Company, Shell, the *Compagnie Française des Pétroles* and a group of five US companies spearheaded by Standard Oil – was essentially co-extensive with the new British client state. To ask which of the two enabled the other is an academic exercise. Granted as a Mandate to the British between 1923 and 1929, Iraq was a crucial front in Britain's ambitious strategy, initiated through the British Controlled Oil Fields Group at the end of World War One, to dominate global oil acquisition. Under pressure from the League of Nations' Covenant to use its mandatory powers to develop representative institutions in Iraq through indirect rule, Britain adroitly cooked up bogus elections, installed a pliant Constituent Assembly and a freshly minted monarch, then successfully rigged a plebiscite with the assistance of its new high commissioner, Sir Percy Fox. With a little help from the League of Nations in 1925, Britain struck a deal with the French to ensure that oil-rich Mosul Province – "Nebuchadnezzar's furnace" – was formally incorporated within Iraq. In short order, a Principal Agreement was signed in March 1931 formally granting the IPC a massive tract of 32,000 square miles of Iraqi territory. A hastily convened Iraqi Parliament rubber stamped what has been called "one of the worst oil deals that has ever been signed",[34] endorsing the IPC demand that no taxes be levied. Iraq surrendered its right to tax the

---

34   US Department of State oil expert Richard Funkhouser, addressing the US National War College in 1951, cited in Francisco Parra, *The Politics of Oil*, London 2004, p. 13.

companies for a "fiscal stability clause", paid for with a trifling one-time payment by the consortium.

Here was the concessionary economy at work. A ramshackle dependency, whose very sovereignty is largely a fiction, grants to an oil company an exclusive right to explore and develop oil over a vast territory for an extended – often indefinite – period of time. The company, armed with full title to all oil resources, operates with total impunity, offering niggardly payments (royalties, rents and taxes) to the host government. As a result of concessions like these, the Big Three oil cartel came to control 70 percent of global oil output by the 1930s. By the end of the Great Depression, the foundations of the modern international oil system – corporate/state collusion, regulation of surplus, and manufactured scarcity by means of interlocking partnerships – had been laid. From the vantage point of the present, the only things missing were drugs and private armies.

The second reality is *America*'s special place in the ongoing story. This turns on the accident of geological history that left the world's largest economy, from the 1920s onward, increasingly dependent on foreign oil. The Persian Gulf figured centrally in America's strategic response.[35] By 1933, Standard Oil of California (SOCAL)[36] had acquired a massive concession from King Ibn Saud, extending from the Persian Gulf to the Red Sea. Within a decade, five US multinationals had invested $1 billion in Iraq, Kuwait, and Saudi Arabia.

---

35 In the wake of the anti-trust break-up of the Rockefeller oil empire, US firms looked further afield to Mexico and Venezuela. The British, French, and Russians meanwhile had excluded US interests from the Ottoman sphere (most dramatically in 1920 when the European powers blocked US concessions in Iraq). American firms pushed hard for an "open door" policy and, under pressure, the British finally succumbed, largely as a result of war debts owed to the US. Jersey Standard and New York Standard were granted access to the old Ottoman lands (and membership in IPC) by Whitehall in 1922.

36 In 1933, SOCAL established the California Arabian Standard Oil Company. In 1943, SOCAL convinced the US government to take over SOCAL's and the British government's funding of the Saudi government. In 1944, SOCAL renamed the company the Arabian American Oil Company (Aramco) and added Exxon and Mobil as co-owners.

The new political cartography of oil had been drawn in full by the end of World War Two. Roosevelt, returning from Yalta in February 1945, met with the Saudi monarch and declared that his country was "more important to US diplomacy than virtually any other nation". Within two years, Truman and his Secretary of State, Dean Acheson, were working directly with Big Oil for strategic assistance. The oil men would provision Europe and the armed forces in Asia (notably Japan and Korea); in return, the oil companies would be given the head of Mosadeq and a military base in Daharan (the center of Aramco's Saudi operations). The coordinates were clear: an inter-state coalition with the Gulf sheiks, an alliance between the military (plus the CIA) and big petroleum, and an international oil system superintended by American firms. From the perspective of the US state's political interests, it was a system and a strategy intended to shore up the Marshall Plan, to exercise "veto power" over Japanese imports, and to help control the spread of Communism in Asia.

The oil system, unstable and rickety at best, needed constant fine-tuning. When in 1968 the British announced their intention to withdraw forces from the Gulf over the next few years, no less than Henry Kissinger stepped in – "to keep Iraq from achieving hegemony in the Persian Gulf".[37] Local forces were to be strengthened in the face of a possible Iraq–USSR alliance.[38] Monarchical rule (Shah Pahlavi in Iran and, as ever, the Saudis) backed by massive military power became the twin pillars of US strategy.

But fine-tuning could not douse the flames of insurgent petro-nationalism. From the very beginning, client states had little control or understanding of price setting. Anglo-Persian, for example, slashed Iranian royalties in 1933 as company revenues tumbled and promptly exiled Reza Shah to South Africa for simply questioning the concessionary

37 Henry Kissinger, *Years of Upheaval*, New York 1982, p. 669.
38 The Ba'athists had broken with the US in 1967 after the Six-Day War, signed a treaty with the Soviets soon after, and nationalized the IPC in 1972.

agreements. Concessions, and the operations of imperial oil, inevitably stoked a strong nationalist reaction. By 1958, John Foster Dulles reluctantly acknowledged the limits of Big Oil geo-strategy, conceding that nationalism "made it more difficult for the oil companies to maintain a decent position".[39] It was Mosadeq in Iran, Abdul Karim Qasim in Iraq, Perez Alfonso in Venezuela, and Abdullah Tariki in Saudi Arabia who emerged as the standard-bearers of national resource control. They cleverly turned to the spot market – the new locus of much international oil trading – with the result that pressures to lower oil prices intensified. In a historic decision, Exxon (formerly Jersey Standard) unilaterally cut posted prices by 10 cents per barrel on August 8, 1960. Harold Snow, the President of British Petroleum, was reported to have wept at the news. There was good reason. OPEC was born a month later as a counter-cartel. The meeting of the five core states in Baghdad seemed to confirm the worst American fears: insurgent nationalism turned into a trade union. Still, OPEC sat dormant for a decade. It was the confluence in 1973 of Libyan radicalism, assertive oil independents, and an Arab oil embargo precipitated by US support for Israel in the Arab–Israeli war, that finally detonated the old system. In a ten-month period in 1974, the price of a barrel of oil rose 228 percent.

The OPEC revolution turned the oil-procurement system upside down. America was now obliged to fashion, from the ruins of the cartel, a new oil strategy in which the Saudi "special relationship" loomed even larger, and had to learn to live with the consequences of something the oil companies had only fantasized: three massive oil price-hikes over the succeeding decade. All of which turned out, unexpectedly, to be good news: for the companies' profitability, for OPEC revenues, and for America's geo-strategic interest in confronting its new economic competitors, Japan and Germany.

---

39   Quoted in D. Little, *American Orientalism*, Chapel Hill 2002, p. 60.

How, then, does this history affect the Blood for Oil argument in the case of Iraq? In brief, we go on to argue the following. First, there was no shortage, or impending shortage, of oil during the time war was in the planning stage. Second, war was in no sense a structural or strategic necessity; indeed, it represented a high-stakes gamble, not least for the oil industry itself. There was a record – long and ignominious – of proven alternatives to military force, as the recent histories of both imperial and American oil reveal. And third, as we have stated previously, a narrow focus on oil *qua* commodity cannot grasp the larger capitalist complex of which oil is a constitutive part. It substitutes oil capital for a wider capitalist nerve center.

IV

We begin with the specter of shortage. Oil is finite, an exhaustible resource. It is no surprise, therefore, that the combination of strategic use and explosive rates of consumption have made the oil sector the object of much Malthusian speculation. Our view is that scarcity and price – the twin sisters of Malthusian pessimism – provide no ground on which the Iraq war can or should be located. The history of twentieth-century oil is *not* the history of shortfall and inflation, but of the constant menace – for the industry and the oil states – of excess capacity and falling prices, of surplus and glut.

It is best to start with the years immediately prior to September 11. Oil prices had in effect collapsed in the late 1990s – a product of the Asian financial crisis and Clinton's Dual Containment policy.[40] A round of corporate mergers, accompanied by a new internal discipline within

40 Brainchild of Martin Indyk, Assistant Undersecretary of State for Near East Affairs, the policy denied Iraq and Iran permission (mostly) to market oil, and allocated their quotas to the Saudis – who in effect were bankrolling the US military presence in the Gulf. The Saudis leapt at the opportunity to increase their quota (indeed to exceed it) as a way of addressing their own economic crisis. By 1997 Saudi Arabia was pumping 8.5 million bpd (in 1985 it had

Photo: Ed Kashi/Corbis

Oil spill, Nembe Creek, Niger Delta, Nigeria, August 2004

OPEC, resulted in prices rebounding to $30 a barrel, but in real terms this was small beer. In response, the 2001 Cheney Task Force did no more than recapitulate an argument made earlier by Jimmy Carter: demand is growing, oil is not scarce, but it is unevenly distributed. Carter had emphasized conservation, at least in the first instance, as a response to market– dependency; Cheney accented military preparedness, national security strategy, and alternate sources of supply (West Africa, the Caspian).

The basic conundrum, again, was to design a system of organized scarcity capable of keeping the oil price low enough for capitalist growth (and latterly, an SUV car culture), and high enough for corporate

been barely 3 million bpd). However, as the Asian contagion spread and economic contraction followed, oil prices collapsed to $9 per barrel in 1998 (see Stephen Pelletiere, *Iraq and the International Oil System*, Washington DC 2004).

profitability and OPEC's Third World "high absorbers".[41] Repeated attempts to *finalize and regularize* these contradictory goals have all proved fruitless: in a sense, post-1945 US oil policy stands in tatters if one simply notes the correspondence between states with oil, political instability, and anti-imperial resistance. Yet oil prices have remained, for almost half a century, *relatively stable (and cheap) in real terms*. Unprecedented price hikes in 1973–74 and 1979–80 had nothing to do with actual oil scarcity, in the same way that the rapid run up in oil prices beginning in March 2004 (to well over $55 a barrel by October 2004) was entirely a matter of what NYMEX traders called "paper froth". Speculators piled into the oil market because hedge funds had no alternatives, and punters wagered on the likelihood of a "supply-disruption premium".[42]

It is true that there has been a recent avalanche of "end of oil" prophecies, connecting to a longer history of apocalyptic thinking about modernity's wholesale dependence upon a finite resource. Oil is running out. The claim is incontestable, of course. The question is when. The Malthusians feed on the opinion of certain hard-rock geologists, Colin Campbell and Kenneth Deffeyes chief among them, who believe that maximum global production is upon us – *now*. There is a new think-tank – the Oil Depletion Analysis Centre – and a lobbying group – the Association for the Study of Peak Oil – devoted to establishing the fact. Yet the vast resources of the new West African "Gulf States", the deep-water fields beginning to be exploited in Mexico and Brazil, the Canadian tar sands, the emergence of Russia as a new oil superpower, and the scramble, however chaotic and violent, in the Caspian – all actively promoted by the Cheney Task Force – point to a rather different world picture.

---

41 High absorbers like Venezuela and Iraq are capable of deploying petro-dollars *internally* for development purposes, and so are much more likely to promote higher prices than surplus-producing low absorbers like UAE or Kuwait.

42 "A burning question", *The Economist*, March 27, 2004, p. 71.

Any response to the scarcity question has to begin with the field of oil statistics, on which there is absolutely no consensus – and sometimes no data.[43] There is disagreement among the oil majors and their organizations (the International Energy Agency, the American Petroleum Institute) about when global oil production is likely to peak – in 2010? 2025? 2045? – and about the production frontier beyond which US security might be endangered. The entire question of company oil reserves is murky – the US Geological Survey and the estimate of oil savant Colin Campbell differ on the subject by 3.9 trillion barrels! – and what figures we have are very likely cooked.[44] The USGS believes Hubbert's Peak is decades away; Royal Dutch-Shell believes it is the other side of 2030; and the US Energy Information Administration places the zenith somewhere between 2021 and 2112. For every King Hubbert there is a Morris Adelman (MIT emeritus professor): over the next half-century, Adelman says, "oil available to the market is for all intents and purposes infinite".[45]

In any case, new technological advances are already opening the way to hugely better recovery rates. Deep-water drilling has exposed hitherto inaccessible fields (in the Gulf of Mexico, the Bight of Benin, Angola, and Brazil). Exploration breakthroughs will continue to redraft the map of energy reserves. Even more radically, the capacity to convert Canadian tar sands into useable hydrocarbons may alone fundamentally refigure the whole geopolitics of petroleum: in time, Canada's reserves could exceed

43 Here is Nicolas Sarkis, Director of the Arab Petroleum Research Center in Paris: "Oil market statistics are fuzzy. Surprisingly OPEC members publish production figures three months late, maintaining the confusion between their theoretical production quotas and actual output …. Operators and observers play hide and seek, attempting to track tankers and consulting secondary sources … to assess daily production". "Is there really a rise in oil prices?", *Le Monde diplomatique*, July 2004, p. 4.

44 Witness the recent debacle at Shell in which the CEO, Sir Philip Watts, was compelled to resign in the wake of corporate downgrading of its West African and Australian reserves. Shell's reserves in Nigeria were apparently overestimated by 15–20 percent largely it appears as a result of a combination of fraud within the Nigerian Petroleum Ministry and a system of tax incentives offered by the government which induced Shell to play fast and loose with its figures in the early 1990s.

45 Morris Adelman cited in V. Vaitheeswaran, *Power to the People*, New York 2003, p. 190.

those of Saudi Arabia. Would not Ottawa be a safer bet as swing producer than Riyadh? Or Baghdad? Even within the energy industry as now constituted, it is gas (liquefied natural gas) that is the new panacea. And the geography of gas reserves is not isomorphic with the geopolitical map of oil security. Finally, there is the vast rearrangement of the energy landscape – studiously ignored by the Cheney Task Force – made possible by new conservation technologies, which in as little as a decade could shift the frontier of oil exhaustion decisively. Sheik Zaki Yamani, Saudi oil minister and one-time head of OPEC, is fond of saying that "the Stone Age did not end for lack of stone".[46] The Oil Age – and with it, hydrocarbon capitalism – will indeed come to an end; but this rubicon will be crossed long before the world runs out of the foul-smelling liquid.

To suggest, then, that absolute scarcity propelled the events of 2003 is untenable. And much the same can be said about price. The relation among so-called "excess demand" (read, ongoing economic expansion), "excess supply" (read, economic recession and improved conservation methods), and price defies any market logic. Over the past three decades, for example, the proxy for availability – the ratio of proven reserves to current production – rose by a quarter, yet in real terms prices doubled. An examination of inventories (a common way to estimate the desires of buyers and sellers) confounds expectations further. During the 1970s, as inventory built up, prices soared; the oil crisis of 1973–74, that is, had nothing to do with shortage – because there was no shortage. By the 1980s, excess consumption had taken hold and inventories diminished, yet, strange to say, prices fell by 71 percent between 1980 and 1986. Over the last fifteen years, the fluctuations of price in relation to excess demand are utterly baffling. The magnitudes of the mismatch between demand and price make little sense. Since 1960, world consumption has typically been 2–3 percent above or below world output. How on earth can such

46 Quoted in V. Vaitheeswaran, *Power to the People*, New York 2003, p. 98.

relatively insignificant discrepancies explain dramatic real-price fluctuations of tens or sometimes hundreds of percent a year? And why are prices sometimes so sensitive to the discrepancies, and other times completely resistant to them?

Why? Because oil is an item (a key item) of market currency, and therefore subject to constantly shifting expectations and perceptions, speculation and gambling – plus the pressure, as always, of "external circumstances". However plentiful supplies have been, since 1960 continual wars and rearmament in the Middle East have generated an atmosphere of crisis. Prices magically return to "acceptable levels" as the conflicts dissipate. But if wars and regional instability produce high prices, the link is in no simple sense causative. The oil industry itself has long built such things into its normal business calculus. The so-called price consensus typically incorporates a "peacetime base", an "embargo effect", and, of course, "war premiums".

If petro-Malthusianism was in some measure a *product* of war, might relative scarcity (concrete threats of supply-disruption) plausibly provide the grounds for invasion? Real oil prices had fallen steadily through the 1990s, and in the wake of world recession were as low as they had been for thirty years. OPEC, as expected, responded (along with Mexico) by cutting output. Saudi Arabia cut its quota by a million barrels, and prices reacted accordingly (amidst some agitation among traders regarding the ascension of Hugo Chavez in Venezuela, and deteriorating US–Iraq relations). Rising oil prices in 2000, and the bursting of the Wall Street high-technology bubble, doubtless fed the perception that oil was scarce and economic recovery might be compromised. But rising oil prices are the reality over the long term (in real dollars, they had doubled in three decades), and they were rising on an historically low base. To suggest that here was a trend that "Americans could barely accommodate"[47] is nonsense.

47 Stephen Pelletiere, *Iraq and the International Oil System*, p. 125.

V

Might the occupation of Iraq nevertheless reflect a deeper morbidity within the entire oil system? Might war have been triggered by short-term capacity problems, or supply disruptions (the nightmare of Osama rocketing oil tankers in the Straits of Hormuz) – maybe with an eye to stability in the long term? Was the resumption of large-scale oil production in Iraq a structural imperative for the stability of the world oil system, or for American capitalism (the strength of the dollar), or for both? In our account, the answer must surely be no.

Let us assume that the Bush oil men *did* see their national and corporate interests undercut by the oil situation worldwide. Let us assume too that the state and the companies were unable or unwilling to compromise on higher but stable prices. Let us take as given that the Administration was incensed by Saddam's switch, in 2000, from dollars to euros in payments received under the Oil for Food program, and terrified that such action might give Iran the same idea. And assume further that French and Russian contracts in Iraq were perceived by the supermajors as undercutting their operations, or their global acquisition strategy. Given all this, why would the companies or the Bush cabinet believe that it required an invasion to put things right? And why might this view have traction on the Left? War, said George Caffentzis,[48] "is the only way for the … oil companies to gain profitable access to Iraqi oil".

"From the point of view of the price of oil" said Adel Beshai, Professor of Economics at the American University in Cairo, "the best thing would be not to attack Iraq at all …. [It] could lead to unpredictable events …. Attack Iraq and you open Pandora's box."[49] The box might

---

48 George Caffentzis, "No Blood for Oil", 2003, http://www.commoner.org.uk/02-9groundzero.htm.
49 Cited in Michael Mann, *Incoherent Empire*, London 2003, p. 209. According to the 2003 *Economist Intelligence Unit*, three quarters of the countries with the "highest risk for foreign investment" are oil producing states.

contain unprecedented price increases, which could be good news for the companies (including non-American majors) – but already, in saying so, we have essentially left the Blood for (Cheap) Oil framework behind. Indeed why open the box at all? The crude art of cutting deals with petro-sharks and oilygarchs was tried and tested. Rumsfeld himself had been such an adept practitioner twenty years earlier – with Saddam and *his* oil men. And had not Cheney at the helm of Halliburton overseen the sale of $22 million of services and parts to Saddam through a subsidiary (Dresser) as part of the notoriously corrupt UN Oil for Food program? It was still all working swimmingly. Why tamper with it? Perhaps to retain the viability of the dollar? If OPEC switched to the euro, might the dollar crash? The dollar has fallen of course, and that is the point. The idea that an OPEC switch could destroy the dollar is implausible; afer all, the cartel accounts for less than 5 percent of cross border capital flows. Perhaps, however, the oil companies were sold a bill of goods, convinced by Cheney and associates that the risk of unforeseen consequences was low. But this is implausible. What the industry wants more than anything else, noted the former Director of Operations for the CIA, is "a stable apple cart".[50] It is a sentiment parroted endlessly by the oil trade press (by late 2001 the trade journals such as *Oil and Gas International* were lamenting the commercial costs of the Afghan invasion). High prices have never compensated for the costs of stabilizing and securing production. All of the supermajors in West Africa – to take one example – have prepared policy papers on the current security situation, and each is haunted by the specter of worsening conditions prompting withdrawal from the region in two to three years.

War is rarely a vehicle for price stability, in other words – but perhaps that is the point. Conflict has been endemic to the industry in the Middle East since the 1960s. And through all the subsequent wars and upheavals

50   Cited in William Engdahl, *A Century of War*, London 2004, p. 268.

– the Arab embargo, the Six-Day War, the Iranian Revolution, the Iran–Iraq conflict, the first Gulf War – oil companies managed to restore their levels of profitability, oil oligarchs and dictators made Switzerland happy, and, in spite of periods of inflationary recession, the oil economy was stabilized. But the 2003 invasion was different – different than the first Gulf War, which had indeed been a struggle over oil supplies.[51] What was on offer to the industry this time was unilateral adventurism in the face of a global Muslim insurgency, and the prospect of enraging the largest generation of young Arabs and Muslims in history. It risked 20 percent of the world's oil supply, the entire Gulf strategy, the wider set of US interests in the region, the radical destabilization of the entire Muslim world, the active promotion of the jihadi struggle, and blowback of a wholly unpredictable and uncontainable sort.

VI

Oil, said a founder of OPEC, is "the devil's excrement". It works magic. It is the force that makes the world go round. In our view, the very formulation of the Blood for Oil hypothesis concedes too much to this magical point of view. As we have said before, it substitutes oil (as one sector of industry) for a dominant capitalist core, and fixes on the character of a single commodity at the expense of the systemic imperatives of capital in general. To grasp this we must return to OPEC and the new oil regime it helped launch.[52]

The 1960s marked a decade-long decline in oil prices, accounted for in part by the unrelenting search for reserves, new upstream technologies,

---

51 Saddam was furious that Kuwait and UAE, under US pressure, were producing over quota to keep prices low. His obvious oil-profits motive elicited widespread condemnation across the Arab world and provided a relatively broad multilateral ground for the American military response.

52 We are deeply indebted to the brilliant analysis of the political economy of oil offered by Jonathan Nitzan and Shimson Bichler in *The Global Political Economy of Israel*, London 2002.

and fresh infusions of oil from Russia, all of which combined to create massive excess capacity. Major new actors appeared on the scene. Old-style collusion was less and less feasible. Against this backdrop, OPEC's politicization of the oil market can be understood not as a threat to the major oil-consuming states but as a new and more sophisticated alignment, resting on a convergence of interest among companies, the US government, and suppliers. A higher price-regime was good for the majors (their profits soared during the 1970s, and their ability to check the power of independents was enhanced), good for Washington (it promised a slowdown in the Japanese and European economies, as Kissinger noted), good for Britain (through North Sea oil and its majors), and good for the Cold War, since it boosted the US military presence in the Middle East. Sheik Yamani articulated OPEC's mission rather well: "to avoid at all costs any clash of interests which would shake the foundations of the whole oil industry".[53]

Big Oil was a beneficiary of the OPEC revolution. But understanding why leads us immediately beyond questions of price and supply to a wider, more inclusive economic – and political – landscape. There is a twofold history at work here. On the one hand, the rollercoaster of price booms and busts, often cutting against long-term trends; and on the other, the ever bleaker epicycles of conflict, militarization and revolutionary upheaval. On the one hand, that is, the *politicization* of the oil sector; on the other, the *commercialization* of the arms industry.[54] This is the heart of the "Weapondollar–Petrodollar Coalition".[55] In the 1950s, 95 percent of US armament exports had been provided as foreign aid.

---

53   Ibid., p. 227.
54   Ibid., pp. 219–73. See also "Transformed: A Survey of the Defense Industry", *The Economist*, July 30, 2002.
55   Nitzan and Bichler, *The Global Political Economy of Israel*, p. 202. According to the Congressional Research Service, the US in 2003 maintained a wide lead in weapon sales ($14.5 billion, 57 percent of the total); Russia ranked (a distant) second. Thom Shanker, "US and Russia still dominate arms market", *New York Times*, August 30, 2004, p. A7. It is perhaps no surprise, then, that Russia accounted for the lion's share of oil contracts in Iraq.

By 2000, the figure had fallen to one quarter. Privatization of the arms trade, naturally, had established itself as the way of the future, and soon the ubiquitous "contractor" was providing everything from air-conditioned tents to morticians. Following a wave of mergers and consolidations in the 1990s (overseen and promoted by the Defense Department), the largest twenty US contractors were reduced to four – Boeing, Northrop Grumman, Lockheed Martin, and Raytheon. Their sales now account for $150 billion, and they control a vast proportion of state contracts. Net profit in the sector, as a share of the total net profit of the Fortune 500, doubled (to 10 percent) between 1965 and 1985. This kind of extraordinary growth of the "Arma-Core" could not be sustained even by US levels of military Keynesianism: it required foreign purchases, and, specifically, Third World buyers.

The key to the rise of the armaments industry – the shift from aid to trade – was the arrival on the scene of OPEC, and the redistribution of global income that followed. In 1963, the Middle East accounted for 9.9 percent of global arms imports; in the decade following 1974, the figure was 36 percent (roughly $45 billion per year).[56] Almost half was provided by US suppliers. According to Nitzan and Bichler, "for every 1 percent change in oil revenues there was, three years later, a 3.3 percent increase in arms imports".[57] The energy conflicts across the region were both cause and consequence of oil-fueled militarization. Endless money, said Cicero, forms the sinews of war.

The Weapondollar–Petrodollar Coalition was sustained by high oil prices (and energy conflicts) but the arrangement was structurally unstable. Excessively high oil prices brought energy substitution and the search for higher-cost non-OPEC oil in their wake; and militarization, should conflicts escalate, might compromise, at any moment, the easy

---

56 Saudi arms imports in 1974 amounted to $2.6 billion; between 1985 and 1992 it spent $52.4 billion. See International Crisis Group, "Can Saudi Arabia Reform Itself?", July 2004, Brussels, p. 27. Web article appearing at www.icg.org.
57 Nitzan and Bichler, p. 233.

complicity of oil companies with the OPEC nerve center. The middle ground, as Nitzan and Bichler see it, was an oil price determined by "tension without war", in which oil corporate profitability stayed ahead of all other major manufacturing sectors. When profits fell to what the industry called a "danger zone", oil men turned hawkish. Each descent into the "danger zone" preceded an energy conflict, and was in turn followed by a dramatic reversal of economic fortune. The price collapse of the 1980s proved to be a major crisis for the new order, compounded by the fact that the Iraq–Iran War – an obvious source of profit – contributed to an oil glut through "distress sales".[58] Added to this, the arms trade during the Reagan era remained subject to foreign policy constraints – as a consequence of which Russia captured 30 percent of the Middle East arms market. The Gulf War and the subsequent defense treaties corrected the disequilibrium, but the 1990s overall proved to be far less welcoming. Oil prices tumbled, oil-producing states (often under neo-liberal pressures) faced domestic austerity, and Arab–Israeli tensions subsided (albeit briefly). A wave of mergers in the oil and armaments industries provided breathing space, but their share of the Fortune 500's capitalization fell to 5 percent. Then along came September 11.

We take our distance here from Nitzan and Bichler's analysis. The kind of political servo-mechanism they point to, precisely calibrating the oil/war nexus – and setting the tempo of American rule more broadly – is in the end too perfunctory, too mechanical. Nevertheless, they point in the right direction. For the significance of oil, we have been arguing, derives as much from the industry's relation to other fractions of capital – to a complex and shifting capitalist epicenter – as from any straight-forward dependence on Gulf reserves. The dialectic of oil and armaments – "build and destroy" – extends, in other words, much

---

58 In 1986 George Bush, then Vice President, went to Riyadh to plead for *lower* levels of oil output by Saudi Arabia, to increase prices and re-stimulate the oil–weapons trade.

further afield, embracing not only military and oil-service industries, but the giants of construction (and "reconstruction"),[59] the global engineering and industrial design sector, and, not least, financial services and banking capital. For these last, the dollar-denominated oil surpluses of the "low absorbers" (Kuwait, UAE, Saudi Arabia) are the necessary raw materials for offshore banking, hedge funds, and speculative capital movements. The OPEC revolution, lest we forget, inserted massive quantities of petro-dollars into the hands of commercial banks, which soon put the money to work – to build and destroy – in Brazil, Argentina, and Mexico.

So it is about Chevron and Texaco, but also about Bechtel, Kellogg, Brown and Root, Chase Manhattan, Enron, Global Crossing, BCCI, and DynCorp. "Oil, Guns and Money" is how Midnight Notes[60] gloss the intersection of work, energy, and war. This comes closest to what we are seeking to emphasize, but even this characterization may be too sanitary, occluding the "black economy" with which the likes of Enron and Halliburton are more and more obviously entangled. Drugs, oil theft, and money laundering are the main activities in this capitalist ghost world; Russia, Nigeria, Colombia, and Mexico the chief way stations. In quantitative terms, these circuits of capital and power are difficult to determine; but they run, almost certainly, to trillions of dollars.

We are not fully convinced that the oil-arms-military-engineering-construction-finance-drugs nexus was brought to crisis point by the "peace dividend", by low oil prices, and by the 1990s explosion of the high-tech sector.[61] But we are confident that a transnational constellation

59 From 1994 to 2002 the Pentagon concluded 3,016 contracts, valued at $300 billion, with twelve private military/service/construction companies; 2,700 went to KBR and the management and technology consulting firm Booz Allen Hamilton.
60 Midnight Notes, *Midnight Oil: Work, Energy, War 1973–1992*, Brooklyn 1992, remains for us an absolutely foundational text for any understanding of the current conjuncture.
61 Nitzan and Bichler believe that the crisis was at hand as early as 1993: gone were the contracts, and gone was stagnation and conflict. As they put it: "civilian business offered much better ways to beat the average" (*The Global Political Economy of Israel*, p. 271).

of capital, anchored through OPEC and the inter-state system, provides the ground on which any argument of corporate interest – the heart of the Blood for Oil thesis – must be assessed. To put the matter in this way does not deny the significance of oil but locates it on a larger capitalist landscape. American empire cannot forgo oil: its control is a geopolitical priority. But these strategic and corporate oil interests cannot, in themselves, credibly account for an imperial mission, however ineptly prosecuted, of the sort we have witnessed over the last two years. Rather, what the Iraq adventure represents is less a war for oil than a radical, punitive, "extra-economic" restructuring of the conditions necessary for expanded profitability – paving the way, in short, for new rounds of American-led dispossession and capital accumulation. This was a hyper-nationalist neo-liberal *putsch*, made in the name of globalization and free-market democracy. It was intended as the prototype of a new form of military neo-liberalism. Oil was especially visible at this moment of extra-economic imposition because, as it turned out, oil revenues were key to the planning and financing of the military exercise itself, and to the reconstruction of the Iraqi "emerging market".

VII

Military neo-liberalism is the key formula, we believe, to a proper determination of the capitalist moment surrounding us, and therefore to the politics of oil. The realities covered by the term "neo-liberalism" hardly need spelling out. The world has endured two decades and more of radical reconstruction made in the name of a new/old capitalist orthodoxy – repeated rounds of privatization and deregulation, tight money (for some), free trade (for the defenseless), "adjustment programs", attacks on welfare and on big (that is, corporate-unfriendly) government. (Ninety-five percent of all regulatory changes during the 1990s, as inventoried by the UN *World Investment Report*, were aimed at liberalizing capital controls. The tripling of bilateral investment treaties in the first half of the same decade was almost wholly aimed at removing "barriers" to foreign investment.) We cannot explore here the origins of neo-liberalism, but they date to the 1970s, and to the challenges confronting US economic hegemony as a result of a crisis of overaccumulation.[62] Faced with growing competition from western Europe, Japan, and East Asia, the US under Richard Nixon dismantled international financial barriers to "liberate the American state from succumbing to its economic weaknesses and … strengthen the political power of the American state"[63]. Institutionally, what permitted this "gamble" of projecting US financial power outwards was the IMF-WTO-Treasury-Wall Street nexus. Right at the heart of neo-liberalism's strategy was an assault on the state-centered development strategies of post-colonial states: markets were to be forced open, capital and financial flows freed up, state properties sold at knockdown prices, and assets devalued and transferred in crises of neo-liberalism's own making. For the Third World, "There is no alternative" was the mantra; for the post-1989 socialist bloc, it was simply dubbed "Shock Therapy". What proved so extraordinary about the neo-liberal counterrevolution was not its missionary zeal, but rather its hyper-nationalism: that a single nation should insist on its own image as a global norm. The 2002 National Security Strategy, we can now see, was its creed, and "full spectrum dominance" its commandment.[64] On balance, the neo-liberal offensive was, as Antonio Gramsci might have put it, a passive revolution from above: conservative, defensive and despotic.

For a while, this version of back-to-the-future seemed to carry all before it. The Fall of the Wall was its emblem; Russian mortality rates and the ruin of Argentina its crowning achievements. The laws of economics,

---

62 Robert Brenner, *The Boom and the Bubble: the US in the World Economy*, London 2002.
63 Peter Gowan, *The Global Gamble*, London 1999, p. 23.
64 See B. Silver and G. Arrighi, "Polanyi's 'Double Movement': The *Belles Epoches* of British and US Hegemony Compared", *Politics and Society*, vol. 31, no. 2, 2003, pp. 325–55.

wrote Lawrence Summers, were "like the laws of engineering". There was only one set, and "they work everywhere". Not for a moment do we underestimate the continuing monochrome allure of such laws over much of the world. But something has clearly shifted in the course of the last ten years. Even as recently as the late 1990s, our masters seemed confident that the new world of capital penetration would come about essentially by means of agreement (between governments and corporations), "fiscal discipline", fine tuning of subsidy and bailout, and nonstop pressure from US creditors. What precise constellation of forces began to put this methodology in question is still open to debate. But it happened – precipitately. Cracks began to appear within the World Bank establishment. Stiglitz fought with Summers, Western Europe fought with the Washington consensus, and the South often refused to take its bitter medicine. The grotesqueries of Third World indebtedness and First World subsidies to corporate agriculture became an issue in polite society. The back-slapping and mutual congratulation of the Uruguay Round descended into the fiasco of Seattle – and the deeper fiascos of Doha and Cancun. At Cancun, what emerged was an in-house insurgency: a Group of Twenty steadfast in its refusal to endorse the massive US–EU subsidies to North Atlantic agriculture, and WTO rules crafted to prevent the South from protecting itself. In the world at large – the world neo-liberalism was fighting to create – struggles accumulated as the price of change became clearer (the Argentine example was much discussed), and capitalism's enemies began to score real successes. The underbelly of "globalization" was now exposed.

This is the proper frame, we believe, for understanding what has happened in Iraq. It is only as part of this neo-liberal firmament, in which a dominant capitalist core begins to find it harder and harder to benefit from "consensus" market expansion or corporate mergers and asset transfers, that the new preference for the military option makes sense. Military neo-liberalism seems to us a useful shorthand for the new reality; but in a sense the very prefix "neo" concedes too much to the familiar capitalist rhetoric of renewal. For military neo-liberalism is no more than primitive accumulation in (thin) disguise.

"Primitive accumulation". The words have an old-fashioned ring to them, which again we think appropriate to the present. They derive, to repeat, from Marx's discussion in *Capital* of the first foundations – the "historic presuppositions" – on which capitalist development in Britain was launched. And what they point to is a history of force, of dispossession and enclosure. We have already quoted the final sentences of Marx's chronicle, and the reader will remember that they put their stress, unforgettably, on the sheer ruthlessness of the history in question. "Blood and fire" are writ large on the landscape.

Marx had no illusions about the role of force in his own time. But he did seem to believe that the age of violent expropriation was at an end. It was capitalism's strength that it had internalized coercion, so to speak, and that henceforward the "silent compulsions of economic relations" would be enough to compel the worker to "sell the whole of his active life".[65] The whiplash of primitive accumulation was required only for the "pretensions of capital in its embryonic state".

We are not the first to think Marx too sanguine (or do we mean too melancholy?) in this diagnosis. For in practice it has turned out that primitive accumulation is an *incomplete* and *recurring* process, essential to capitalism's continuing life. This is true in at least two senses. First of all, the class of small landed laborers – modernity's sacrificial lambs – has proven remarkably resilient, and still fights for survival in the twenty-first century. The collapse (or reform) of "actually existing socialisms" over the past two decades produced several hundred million *new* peasants as the millennium drew to a close. If accumulation depends, as Marx said, on the multiplication of a true proletariat, then the obstacles to the creation of such uniformity never quite seem to go away.

65 Karl Marx, *Capital*, vol. 1, pp. 899–900.

The process is incomplete in another sense: namely, that it is not simply the dispossession of labor(ers) that is key to primitive accumulation, but *all* forms of dispossession. And these forms recur, and reconstitute themselves, endlessly: the reconstitution is fundamental to capitalism as a system. "The original sin of simple robbery", as Hannah Arendt put it, must "be repeated lest the motor of accumulation suddenly die down".[66] Hence the periodic movement of capitalism outward, to geographies and polities it can plunder almost unopposed. (Or so it hoped, in the case of Iraq.) But hence, also, its drive *inward*, deep into the fabric of sociality, in search of resources to rip from the commons. How else, for example, to grasp the present reality of the patenting of life-forms? How else to make sense of the myriad ways in which collectively held goods and resources are privatized – pension funds, basic utilities, public housing, forests once open to shared use? And how better to bring into focus the periodic financial crises or structural adjustment programs – perpetrated by the IMF and other global regulatory institutions, by hedge funds, or by concerted campaigns of speculation – that bring in their wake a wholesale devaluation of wealth, and across-the-board transfer of assets from local to foreign hands?[67]

The question remains, of course, as to why the process of primitive accumulation takes on, as it regularly does, a specifically military (imperialist) form. An answer in general is easy to find. However dispersed and ingenious its procedures may be in each new instance, primitive accumulation is essentially an exercise of violence. Blood and fire are its vectors. All forms of primitive accumulation, said Marx, *require* "the power of the state". Force is, he said, both the midwife of the new and itself an economic power.[68] So the state hovers always in the wings. But what are

---

66 Hannah Arendt, *The Origins of Totalitarianism*, New York 1958 (orig. pub. 1951), p. 182.
67 See David Harvey, *The New Imperialism*, London 2003, *passim,* especially his discussion of "accumulation by dispossession".
68 Karl Marx, *Capital*, vol. 1, p. 751.

the circumstances, precisely, which oblige the state to land on stage, in the way it has lately? They are rarely, *contra* Marx, straightforwardly "economic". In the past few years, it is the interweave of compulsions – spectacular, economic, geopolitical – that reveals American empire's true character.

Will military neo-liberalism endure? Indeed, what might victory under current circumstances consist of? With the deficit rolling along at $600 billion annually, and the national debt rising to $2.5 trillion, the cost-benefit balance of the strategy begins to look dubious. No doubt many state functionaries are doing their sums. And what of Operation Iraqi Freedom? Two years after the tanks rolled across the Euphrates floodplain, the occupation barely has control of Baghdad. With unemployment running at perhaps 50 percent, the Mahdi Army steadily draws new support from the ranks of the urban unemployed in the slums of Sadr City and Basra, now twice dispossessed: once by Saddam, once by Bush. The estimated number of insurgents has risen from two to over twenty-five thousand. It all "continues to calm down", said Rumsfeld in August 2004.

Even the luster of the privatized contract economy has tarnished. Of the $18.4 billion in reconstruction funds allocated by the US Congress in October 2003, less than 9 percent has been spent a year later – and untold amounts of that on "security". During the same period, 113 criminal investigations of contractors have been launched by one Congressional agency alone, and cases opened on another 272 allegations of fraud and "waste".[69] As if to confirm the falling rate of expectations, Halliburton is reportedly putting Kellog, Brown and Root on the block because it has become so unprofitable. So much for the Great Iraqi Oil Robbery. Even Rumsfeld admits "we lack metrics to know if we are winning or losing the war".[70] And however you calculate it, in the present equation a few more million barrels of oil will not matter a damn.

69 *Washington Post*, November 1, 2004.
70 Cited in Alan Krueger and David Laitin, "Misunderstanding Terror", *Foreign Affairs*, 83/5, 2004, p. 13.

3

PERMANENT WAR

Hobbes's insistence on power as the motor of all things human …
sprang from the theoretically indisputable proposition that never-
ending accumulation of property must be based on a never-ending
accumulation of power …. The limitless process of capital accumulation needs the political structure of so "unlimited a Power"
that it can protect growing property by constantly growing more
powerful.

—Hannah Arendt, *The Origins of Totalitarianism*

To what extent did September 11, and the American state's responses to
it, usher in a new geopolitical era? This is a question about empire. It
leads to another: To what extent have the events of September 11
obliged – and provided an opportunity for – American capital and its
state executor to embark on a fresh phase of imperial business as usual?
We take up these questions here, this time by examining the historical
trajectory of US militarism.

So far in the book, our key terms of analysis have been spectacle and
capital. There is a third aspect to the present reality – war (and its ghostly
double, peace). And the concepts "war" and "the state", as Randolph
Bourne never tired of arguing, are deeply linked – in a sense, mutually
constitutive. This is one aspect of the story that follows. Another is the

link between war and modernity. For nothing could be more mistaken than to take the recrudescence of war in the present conjuncture as part of a turn to the past. World War Two was already a twenty-four-hour, mechanized conflict coordinated by remote control and the embryonic technics of the computational and the virtual, whose flourishing in due course made possible a new stage – a new pervasiveness – in the image-management of society. The whole cyberworld, in consequence, bears the marks of its origin in the needs and fantasies of Central Command. The Revolution in Military Affairs is recognizably the highest (we should say, the quintessential) achievement of the "information age".

War, in a word, is modernity incarnate. It is the force that has engendered, and given specific form to, the technical powers now at our disposal. And we shall only properly grasp these powers' partiality – what they are capable of, and what human capacities and possibilities they are dedicated to annulling – if we return to the real world from which they issued. The world of empire, that is, and "the pursuit of politics by other means". It may even be that the famous phrase from Clausewitz is a touch too optimistic. For war, thus far in human history, has not been an "other", or optional, means of political conduct. It has been what politics most fully and essentially is. This is the story we mean to tell in what follows – not in order to intimidate or demoralize the "peace movement", but to put it in mind of the enormity it aims to oppose.

I

The American state's most salient post-September 11 responses have been invasion and military occupation in Afghanistan and Iraq. In reaction, many voices have contended that the post-September 11 moment – in the brushing aside of national sovereignty, superannuation of the United Nations, completing the computerization of warfare, or the seizure of power by a cabal in the White House basement – marks the beginning of a new age in the militarization of politics. We will argue, to the contrary, that these invasions and occupations are, for the most part, of a piece with an almost unbroken line of imperial American military interventions, stretching back almost two hundred years. That is, rather than an historical rupture, they mark the elevation – into a state of *perma-nent war* – of a long and consistent pattern of military expansionism in the service of empire. Moreover, we will argue that the pretexts trundled out as cover for this most recent phase in the imperial project likewise fit within a long-standing set of legitimizing casuistries.

Military excursions have served as the primary strategic element in a history of relentless imperial expansion – from the Monroe Doctrine of 1823 through the Cold War to the present. September 11 both prodded and emboldened the state to commence the next series of moves in an established expansionist pattern, facilitated by – and facilitating – an ever-increasing US military presence throughout key regions of the world, and by the structures of fealty and dependence such a presence establishes. As Donald Rumsfeld immediately saw it (proposing the inva-sion of Iraq within days after the World Trade Center attacks), September 11 "created the kind of opportunities that World War Two offered, to refashion the world".[71]

This is not to deny, however, that the American state is now sailing into uncharted, highly treacherous waters. It is groping to manufacture an adequate reply to the spectacular defeat of September 11. More generally, the state feels the need, both strategic and spectacular, to respond to the unbearable dispersion beyond nation-states of the means of mass violence. In this regard, the "regime change" operations against state powers in Afghanistan and Iraq have only momentarily veiled the incoherence of US efforts to put the weapons genie back in the bottle. And these new killing-fields have again created conditions in which

71 *New York Times*, October 12, 2001.

non-state forces are gaining momentum, adherents, and the military wherewithal to deliver the next round of blows.

The long-cherished fiction of America as the "reluctant power" has been utterly abandoned since September 11. If the invasion of Iraq, by barely prepared forces clearly lacking sufficient allies, was not evidence enough of American eagerness for martial aggression, the 2002 National Security Strategy's frank declaration of intent – its prospective self-vindication for the use of preemptive, unilateral force – clinches the case. In this new explicit posture, however, the ideological frames used to explain its aggression become vulnerable: regarding Iraq, "terrorism", "weapons of mass destruction", and "human rights" are already stretched to transparency. And without such covering tissue, the American state may have difficulty maintaining the level of passivity required of a domestic population already restive under the shocks of neo-liberal policies turned back on the homeland.

What we shall picture here is no smoothly gliding imperial machine, but rather a clumsy, lurching apparatus, responding contingently, and by no means moving in a single direction. Nevertheless, the different, even competing, vectors – any combination of which may at some point gather sufficient weight to propel the US into a new aggression – ultimately present American empire with tactical rather than strategic decisions. That is, despite often inchoate rationales and uncontrollable specific outcomes (including some ignominious retreats[72]), each military intervention is intended to serve an overall strategic project of pressing American power – and the potential for Western capital entrenchment in "emerging markets" – ever further into vital regions of the globe. It is the constant pressure exerted by this project that provides the impetus – with which particular and local interests combine at different, often seemingly random, moments – to push the war machinery into action.

---

72 Notably, the early-twentieth-century occupation of the Philippines, Lebanon, Somalia, and Vietnam.

At the same time, the repeated use of military force, to whatever immediate end, serves also to normalize itself, and to *keep the machine running*. Any analysis that claims a single *casus belli* to explain the war on Iraq, or indeed any given intervention, without paying full heed to the momentum of this thoroughly militarized, deep strategic project, will be fundamentally incomplete. Before examining the current components of American imperial militarism, therefore, we have to bare the historical foundation on which it rests.

II

Military expansionism by the American state begins as soon as the US displaces Britain from its position as hegemon of the northwest Atlantic. Once the War of 1812 had ended the last serious British designs on the Atlantic side of sub-Canadian North America, the US utilized its newly enhanced and professionalized armies to begin a period of rapacious expansion. This early reach to the south and west was intended to provide the US with vast tracts of agricultural land. But it was the quest for markets to service this increasingly *commercial* agrarian economy that pushed the arc of American control further and further afield.

General Andrew Jackson's preemptive military strikes into Florida quickly brought about capitulation by Spain – which was preoccupied with rebellions in South America – and sale of the territory to the US in 1819. The following decade saw intense rivalry among Britain, Spain, France, and the US over the vast resources and markets of newly independent South American states, and among the US, Russia, and Britain for what eventually became the American Northwest. In 1823 President James Monroe rebuffed diplomatic alliances regarding these potential spoils, and issued a belligerent proclamation that all of the Americas was now off-limits to the European powers. The Monroe Doctrine threatened preemptive military action in response to any European challenge to its planned hegemony in the Western Hemisphere: "Interposition" in Latin America by any European state would lead to an American riposte "indispensable to their [the newly independent nations'] security". And for domestic consumption, the proclamation conjured the first in a long line of chimerical "threats" to the US: any European attempt to unduly influence the "destiny" of any Latin American state would be viewed as "the manifestation of an unfriendly disposition toward the United States … dangerous to our peace and safety".

Destiny and its scriptural echoes were everywhere audible in the rhetoric of expansion over the next several decades. As the US digested the vast Louisiana and Florida territories it had added in the first quarter of the nineteenth century (accelerating in the process the mass slaughter and displacement of American Indian populations), the eyes of American capital turned to the Pacific Coast, and to the immense Asia trade which might flow through its ports. The "Panic of 1837" intensified the search for new foreign markets, at the same time as the new steam-driven rail and river networks (linked by the telegraph) powered further expansion westward.

President James Polk oversaw an intensive period of aggressions in the direction of the Pacific, including the annexation of Texas (1845), and a war with Mexico (1846) resulting in US sovereignty over California. This American demonstration of willingness to wage war on the continent forced Britain to cede the Oregon territory to the US, and compelled the French and Spanish to back away from the Yucatán. The ideological mantle for these aggressions was the closed, deadly logic of "Manifest Destiny": that it is good and proper for America to make use of its might; and, conversely, that if the US does so, it must be for the good. Note how the credo played on the notion of America as God's own and only state; and in its references to the defense of "humanity" and the "rights" of conscience we glimpse the prehistory of military humanism:

In its magnificent domain of space and time, the nation of many nations is destined to manifest to mankind the excellence of divine principles; to establish on earth the noblest temple ever dedicated to the worship of the Most High – the Sacred and the True. Its floor shall be a hemisphere – its roof the firmament of the star-studded heavens, and its congregation an Union of many Republics, comprising hundreds of happy millions ....

It is our unparalleled glory that we have no reminiscences of battle fields, but in defense of humanity, of the oppressed of all nations, of the rights of conscience, the rights of personal enfranchisement.[73]

How direct the line from this remarkable piece of nineteenth-century dissimulation – by a slave-holding nation continuing the genocide of Native Americans and about to commence a war of annexation against Mexico – to the pieties of contemporary American ideologues: "Freedom and fear are at war, and we know that God is not neutral between them".[74]

The Civil War and recovery from it put further territorial acquisition temporarily on hold. But the pace of industrialization spurred by the war meant that expanding markets were now crucial to the health of American capital. At first, the remnants of the Union army were used solely to reinvigorate the push west to the Pacific Coast, completing along their way the crushing of native populations. But soon the rich resources, cheap labor supply, and potential markets of the Caribbean and Latin America – as well as control over the planned Panama canal – proved too tempting. President William McKinley deployed the Monroe Doctrine as the centerpiece of propaganda for the Spanish–American War of 1898. Along with the "threat" reprise, centered on the sinking in

---

73 Texas politician and editor John L. O'Sullivan's original text iteration of Manifest Destiny in "The Great Nation of Futurity", vol. 6, issue 23 (1839), pp. 426–30.
74 George W. Bush, Address to Joint Session of Congress, September 20, 2001.

Havana harbor of the battleship *Maine* – a sort of pelagic Twin Towers – it was saving "our little brown brothers" (McKinley) from Spanish oppression that was offered to explain the US annexation of Puerto Rico, Guam, and the Philippines, and the occupation of Cuba. The war also served as cover for the annexation of Hawaii, which had been a Dole Company "republic" since 1893.

Though the Spanish–American War was a broad success for American militarism, its aftermath presented US empire with specific new challenges, as a result of which the modern American imperial structure took shape. It was immediately apparent in Cuba, and soon became clear in the Philippines, that Old World-style colonization – permanent occupation and direct rule – was unmanageable: too costly, too unwieldy, and in the Philippine case requiring an open-ended, brutal and bloody (a half-million or more Philippine deaths) repression. Traditional colonies, already seen to be gravely sapping European powers, needed replacing. What emerged was a form of indirect control which established the lineaments of twentieth-century American imperialism: invasion, often preceded by massive bombardment primarily intended to terrorize and "pacify" the civilian population; the establishment of long-term US military encampment, and the build-up, corruption, and subordination of the local military; and, in the "peace" that follows, reconstruction into a new (weak) state, under terms dictated by the US and its corporate clients. The new polity is then administered by local elites, whose brutalities substitute for those of the withdrawing American power.

Using this new formula, the Platt Amendment (1901) set terms for the independence of Cuba which was to follow the exit of American troops: Cuba "consented" to an ongoing US right to intervene militarily – which it did four more times by 1920. And to further enable the US "to maintain the independence of Cuba", the US entitled itself to lease such Cuban lands as were necessary to establish American naval bases (the origins of US sovereignty over Guantanamo Bay).

In 1903 the US military landed in Colombia to facilitate the "independence" of what was to become Panama, and thereby secured control over land for the canal. It did so under a new statement of military belligerence now referred to as the Roosevelt Corollary (1904) to the Monroe Doctrine: as a "civilized nation", the US had the right to military intervention anywhere in the Western Hemisphere to stop "chronic wrongdoing" – nominally including foreign meddling but primarily meaning resistance to American-supported oligarchies by local populations.[75] A few years later the US invoked the Corollary while invading Nicaragua (1912) to secure the American agribusiness, mining, and transport interests which had controlled and looted the local economy for a half-century – what President Taft at the time unblushingly referred to as the exercise of "dollar diplomacy". US Marines remained for twenty years in Nicaragua as "international police" to prop up local *commandantes*. And in a precursor of the oil-money-for-reconstruction scam in Iraq, US banks were granted control over all Nicaragua's customs collections, and the money used to pay off national "debts" to US corporate interests.

Conventional accounts of President Woodrow Wilson draw a portrait radically unlike that of his martial predecessors: a lean and somber intellectual, preaching first American "neutrality", then (reluctantly) warfare to "make the world safe for democracy" and for "self-determination of peoples". Behind the Presbyterian cant, however, Wilson carried on the American imperial project full force, sending waves of troops to pacify Haiti (1915) and enforce a customs receivership there like the one in Nicaragua; to punish insurgents in Mexico (1916); and to occupy the Dominican Republic (1916) – all in the run-up to America's first foray into the European motherland.

---

75 "Chronic wrongdoing" by Latin Americans is still on the military plate. Head of the US Southern Command General James Hill, testifying (March 24, 2004) before the House Armed Services Committee, complained about being left out of the recent flash-flood of cash to the military for the War on Terror. But we have "radical populists", he volunteered, "You know, 'emerging' terrorists".

Following the mass slaughter of World War One, an overwhelming societal battle fatigue led to a period of relative military quiescence for the US, as had happened in the years immediately after the Civil War. During the 1920s, "Pan Americanism" – military and economic support for compliant Latin American and Caribbean ruling classes, in their efforts to control the local populations – proved a workable alternative strategy, though US military forces were still busy in the region: well into the 1930s, the Marines and Navy continued to occupy Nicaragua and the Dominican Republic, and to enforce the US hijacking of customs payments in Haiti. Capital's great crisis of the 1930s, however, and Japan's growing threat to a free American hand in East Asia, meant that for the US the time of imperial retrenching would be short-lived.

III

The still prevailing reading of the Cold War, even among commentators on the Left, is of an ideologically driven US military, arrayed throughout the world as a defensive bulwark to contain Communist expansion. And indeed, the attempt to establish and maintain ideological advantage was a major factor in the evolution of particular Cold War aggressions – the US- and Saudi-funded *mujahidin* in Afghanistan being a prime example. But the notion of a primarily "defensive" American state during the Cold War is exposed as vaporous by even a cursory look at the crucial years following World War Two.

Rising post-war unionism, plus a deep recession in 1949, had plunged American capital into crisis. President Harry Truman, with Secretary of State Dean Acheson and shadow secretary John Foster Dulles, responded by crafting a new military Keynesian strategy, encapsulated in the notorious National Security Council Report 68 (April 1950). A vast increase in military spending was to be combined with a policy of aggressive military engagements and emplacements across the globe – essentially militarizing all international relations, and thereby solidifying the Pentagon's role as a prime engine of domestic and global capital expansion. Within three months of NSC 68, the US was dispatching hundreds of thousands of troops into Asia, ostensibly to support the new Korean War effort. "Korea saved us", said Secretary Acheson. "Korea has been a blessing", said General Van Fleet. "There had to be a Korea either here or some-place else."[76] Nonetheless, with the US military still occupying the moral high ground in the aftermath of World War Two, and with the ideology of anti-Communism operating both to rationalize the war and to bludgeon what little domestic dissent appeared, few made the connection between the Korean War and the newly emerging Asian markets.

Within the larger project of militarizing an expansionist foreign policy, the Korean War was crucial to the establishment of vast permanent mili-tary complexes throughout Asia (begun in 1945 with the occupation of Japan). Under cover of the Korea "police action", the US military budget tripled in only two years. Most of this massive increase, however, went not to prosecute the war in Korea but to increase the number of US bases throughout the world, and to build a nuclear stockpile. As part of this strategic turn, the US picked up the pace of aggression and military entrenchment across the globe. The list of Cold War-era US interven-tions – a lethal combination of invasion, incursion, and coup-support – is dizzying: overthrow of the Mosadeq government in Iran (1953); staging of a coup in Guatemala (1954); Marines landing in Lebanon (1958); dispatch of 20,000 troops to the Dominican Republic (1965); overthrow of the civilian government in Indonesia (1965); defeat of Allende in Chile (1973); proxy war in Nicaragua (1970s–80s); "civil war" in El Salvador (1980s); another incursion into Lebanon (1982–83); invasion of Grenada (1983); invasion of Panama (1989).

---

76   Speaking to a political delegation from the Philippines in January, 1952, quoted in I. F. Stone, *The Hidden History of the Korean War*, New York and London 1952, p. 348.

Most gruesome of all, of course, was the project to gain control of Southeast Asia. The assault on Indochina should remind us – hearten us – how close to the edge of failure the empire's militarized logic sometimes operates. US entry into Vietnam and Laos in the early 1960s filled a vacuum left by French colonial retreat. Initial intervention consisted of the familiar mix of money, arms, and military trainers, deployed in support of local cadres. (The recipe proved brutally successful during the same period in Indonesia – with the accompanying deaths of several hundred thousand.) Having miscalculated the depth and strength of resistance in Vietnam, however, the American military soon moved to a second stage – a sharp increase in military "advisers" on the ground and carpet-bombing from above. And finally to massive commitment of troops.

When all of these tactics ultimately proved inadequate, the American state was faced with a double loss: the material failure to gain a bridgehead on the southern Asian mainland, and a defeat on the terrain of the spectacle. The war in Asia had nothing to do with "containment": there was no serious threat of Soviet control over Vietnam or Laos – Southeast Asia was instead in the bailiwick of China, which had just broken with the Soviets, and was too preoccupied by internal struggles to pose a direct threat. No, what haunted American leaders – and what led them to continue the carnage long after it had ceased making strategic sense – was the prospect of defeat, coupled with mutinous barracks and a riotous home front, becoming a worldwide televised *image* of failure. As it now haunts them again, from the back streets of Fallujah, Najaf, and Baghdad.

IV

In the decade following the end of the Cold War, the US engaged in a nearly continuous barrage of aggressions. By the year 2000, the annual US military budget was greater than that of Russia, China, all European

NATO states, and Israel *combined*. About 27 percent (roughly $450 billion) of the federal budget in 2000 went to current military spending, and another 15 percent or so ($200–240 billion) on related residual expenses (pensions, plus interest on the national debt attributable to military expenditures – figures the government never includes in its official military budget statistics). Bear in mind, all this was *before* the invasions and occupations of Afghanistan and Iraq, and the massive outlays on "homeland security". Before September 2001, the US already deployed some 285,000 troops and Pentagon personnel in at least 130 countries around the world. And these figures fail to include either the militarized operatives of the many US spy agencies, or the rapidly increasing numbers of civilian "security" subcontractors – mercenaries – now so much in favor. By 2001, there were over 700 officially recognized US military bases around the world, not including numerous secret installations and de facto US facilities operating under local flags of convenience. The post-Cold War US project had also become thoroughly dependent on exchanges, training, and exercises undertaken directly with the officer corps of armies around the globe (in over 100 countries in 2000). Not to mention the trade in arms: at this point the US sells over 50 percent of all the weapons put into circulation in the world market.

The past ten years of interventions have displayed a certain tactical variety – but strategically, the logic has been unchanging. The 1990–91 Gulf War provided Bush Senior with a much-needed, if ultimately futile, surge in domestic political support. But the war served solid imperial ends: it gave the Pentagon an opportunity to establish and expand its bases in the Gulf, to demonstrate its willingness and ability to use direct force in the region, and to begin the debilitation of Iraq. In the Clinton years, between 1993 and 2000, the enforcement of sanctions and the ceaseless air war on Iraq served to justify the need for US troop strength in the Gulf, while continuing to "soften" the Iraqi military and state apparatus, preparatory to invasion. The relentless bombing of Iraq also normalized in the American public mind the notion of making war there; when full-scale war was finally launched, the US public was ready to accept even the flimsiest of pretexts.

These broad objectives notwithstanding, the bombings also served particular parochial interests. For example, the Clinton administration's June 1993 missile attack on central Baghdad had no immediate cause or purpose other than to demonstrate Clinton's "mettle", and to win him Pentagon support early in his presidency. Similarly, in September 1996 the US launched a series of missile attacks after Iraqi forces attacked Kurds in the north; the military knew well that this bombing would be of no tactical help to the Kurds, but again it served to normalize "punishment" of Saddam without risking American casualties.

The 1992–93 intervention in Somalia presented a similar mix of the tactically chaotic with the strategically consistent, though with an outcome that prefigured (on a smaller scale) the spectacular defeat of September 11. Bush Senior sent 25,000 troops to the immiserated, but strategic, Horn of Africa; "humanitarian relief" provided the cover for this massive emplacement, since neither the Pentagon nor the politicians could come up with even the faintest simulacrum of a threat to the US. In spring 1993, Clinton sent still more troops to Somalia, in an attempt to alchemize an entirely new state apparatus in thrall to the US – much like the current bunkered "governing councils" in Afghanistan and Iraq. (Somalia was also an early instance of the US bullying the UN into providing a fig-leaf "international community" cover.) The Somalia occupation spun out of control, however, with US casualties, large numbers of Somalis killed by US troops, and finally the internationally televised horror show of "Blackhawk Down" – the mutilated body of a US soldier being dragged in front of exultant crowds. Withdrawal followed in a matter of weeks. The images of failure and degradation in Somalia prefigured, in a minor way, the September 11 attacks: the US's new "smart" bombs dropped on Iraq, Sudan, and the Balkans throughout the remainder of the 1990s were intended, in part, to erase the memory of spectacular defeat in Mogadishu.

The Balkans was the other theater of major US bloodletting in the 1990s. After four years without direct American engagement in the civil war there, in 1995 Clinton ordered the bombing of Bosnian Serbs. There was no real tactical objective, since his State Department was at the same moment scuttling the Dayton peace talks. But the bombing did serve the larger strategic interests of the empire: a year after the Somalia retreat, it demonstrated renewed US resolve to use its military; and it reasserted US military authority over NATO, and thus over Europe, while pushing the NATO envelope east, "out of area", thereby setting the stage for further US interventions under NATO insignia.

The decade ended with Clinton ordering the massive bombardment of Kosovo and Serbia in the name of humanitarian aid for Albanian Kosovars. The bombs did little to stop Serb atrocities in Kosovo itself, and indeed led to a new round of ethnic bloodletting unleashed on Kosovan Serbs by returning elements of the US-armed "Kosovo Liberation Army" (the right-wing ethnic-Albanian nationalist militia described elsewhere by the CIA and State Department as a "terrorist" organization). As many commentators have since demonstrated, Milošević was ready to withdraw *before* the bombing campaign, and was only prevented by the US continually changing the terms on which he was to capitulate. And without a US willingness to reconstitute the economy or civil society in Kosovo, the bombardment left the tiny region in a desperate shambles, which is how it remains more than five years later.

Despite these tactical incoherencies – not to mention the thousands of civilian Kosovars (on both sides) and Serbs on whose heads the bombs were dropped indiscriminately – the military campaign continued. The appearance of assistance to Muslim Kosovars was intended to play well in Turkey, and across the Gulf region, as the US geared up for its next moves there. The war once again showcased the "demonstration effect" of bringing down an intransigent political leader (Milošević entered the rogues' gallery, alongside the other recent inductees, Noriega and Saddam). But perhaps most significantly, and regardless of the campaign's devastation of the country, it permitted the US for the first time to entrench its military in the Balkans: the massive (and massively fortified) Camp Bondsteel in Kosovo itself, and new bases in the suddenly welcoming Albania, Croatia, Macedonia, Romania, and Bulgaria.[77] Connecting with Turkey, this line of military encampments provides a direct bridge between Europe and the Caspian and beyond into Central Asia, and closer staging-grounds for strikes into the Middle East. Not incidentally, these new bases also permit the withdrawal of huge numbers of troops from Germany – a prudent move, given the country's increasingly refractory populace. And the Kosovo campaign also tested the waters for a US military intervention without even the pretense of UN approval – waters into which it would dive deep only three years later.

V

We have aimed to establish here the structural template of American imperial expansion, against which in turn the ongoing wars in Afghanistan and Iraq can be viewed. Regardless of the tactical details of various invasions, occupations, and retreats, the US empire has followed a long and consistent strategic path – centered on and driven by military engagement – to force regional penetration and exploit the existing or resulting "weak states". And throughout this history, certainly no less so over the past several decades, what passes for "peace" has prefigured – has been *structured* to prefigure – an endless series of wars.

---

77 Camp Bondsteel is situated directly on the route chosen for the long-planned AMBO trans-Balkan oil pipeline, as well as "Corridor 8" of a proposed vast pan-European transport and communications network.

We want to emphasize here how the reality of permanent war renders inadequate the notion of "peace" as an oppositional frame or strategy, and puts paid to the purported difference between an American state in the hands of a "war party" as opposed to a "party of peace". Let us put our case conditionally: Unless the anti-war movement comes to recognize the full dynamics of US militarism – to understand that peace, under current arrangements, is no more than war by other means – then massive mobilizations at the approach of full-dress military campaigns must inevitably be followed by demoralization and bewilderment.

A reminder about the 1990s: that decade *between* wars had meant, through sanctions, a million Iraqi deaths, more or less – during peace, no one bothers to count – from starvation and disease. And not only sanctions: the bombing never stopped. Between July 1997 and January 1999 alone, American aircraft flew 36,000 sorties over Iraq. After eight years of decimation from the air, Iraq was now "lacking in assets", a phrase that points to the deep historical connections between state terror and imperial peace. "They make a desert and call it peace": the great quote from Tacitus still drives to the heart of the matter. States are deeply war machines, and the peace they make is the peace of *pacification*. Always they are in search of better ways to make a desert.

In this long history, the tactic of choice has been, overwhelmingly, terror from the air. No sooner was the chemical formula for gunpowder published in China in 1044 than the contest began to devise the most deadly casings for it, and the most efficient delivery systems. The fragmentation bomb was a fifteenth-century Chinese device – shells filled with shards of porcelain for the maiming of "soft targets" – reinvented in 1784 by Henry Shrapnel. European historians are pleased to call the hundred years between Waterloo and the Somme the "long peace", but this was a century in which the area of the world under European imperial control grew from 35 percent to 85 percent – a theft made

'They make a desert …', Fallujah, Iraq, November 2004

possible, in large part, by bombardment of undefended towns and cities. The century's catalogue of incendiary pacification is staggering. In 1854 an American naval bombardment destroyed San Juan del Norte in Nicaragua. The British protested the bombing of a city without defenses, but two years later they burned down Canton in exactly the same way, and in 1863 destroyed the Japanese city of Kagoshima with an offshore bombardment. Valparaiso in Chile was similarly devastated in 1866 by the Spanish Navy; Alexandria razed in 1882 by British Navy shelling: "During the night the city was transformed into a sea of fire".[78]

At the 1899 peace conference at the Hague – when the Wright brothers were still tinkering on the ground, only dreaming of flight – it was already well understood that the most serious threat to civilians came from the air. When the "small countries" argued for the total prohibition of air war, the imperial powers baulked, with Lord Wolseley putting the British case. The line of argument, revealing his lordship as absolutely modern, was both humanitarian (bombing would "shorten the length of the campaigns") and progressive ("Restrictions on scientific inventions deprive a nation of the advantages which accrue from its scientific men and from the productive capacity of its manufacturing establishments").[79]

In 1924, the infamous Air Marshal "Bomber" Harris, then a young squadron leader in the Iraq air campaign, wrote: "The Arab and Kurd now know what real bombing means in casualties and damage. They know within 45 minutes a full-sized village can be nearly wiped out and a third of its inhabitants killed or injured". One of Harris's colleagues added: "Air control is a marvelous means of bringing these wild mountain tribes to heel. It is swift, economic and humane."[80]

The logic of aerial bombardment as delivery of state terror – wholly

---

78 Sven Lindqvist, *A History of Bombing*, New York 2000, p. 18.
79 Quoted in D. C. Watt, "Restraints on War in the Air before 1945", in Michael Howard (ed.), *Restraints on War: Studies in the Limitation of Armed Conflict*, New York 1979, p. 117.
80 Quoted in S. M. Menon, "Iraq – 'Terror Bombing', Starvation and Mechanical Force", *Economic and Political Weekly*, January 2–9, 1999.

apart from tactical military purpose – reached apocalyptic extremes in World War Two. There were over forty cubic meters of rubble for every inhabitant of Dresden.[81] The figure for Tokyo was never calculated, though it would have been an appropriate job for Robert McNamara, then a junior statistician on the staff of General Curtis Lemay, tasked with creating an optimally efficient firestorm over Tokyo and sixty-six other Japanese cities. The business of managing the post-1945 peace was put in the hands of the new institutions of post-war capitalism, the IMF and the World Bank, to which McNamara – paradigmatic accountant/hit-man for the new militarized neo-liberalism – was to move directly after his time at Harvard Business School and the Ford motor company, and as overseer of the carpet-bombing of Southeast Asia. Capital's post-1945 strategy was conducted within the peace established in the days following the destruction of Hiroshima and Nagasaki, a permanent peace *as pacification*, under the shadow of the atomic bomb.

The record, then, is clear. Preemptive terror by shell, rocket, and bomb is at the core of nineteenth- and twentieth-century imperialism. Peace and terror are, from the perspective of imperialists and civilizers, inextricable. How could this fact – that airborne terror has been a central "pacifying" experience for millions of modern humans – surprise anyone at the beginning of the twenty-first century? And yet this is one of the triumphs of the spectacle: that despite the mushroom cloud and the "smart bomb" – or perhaps because of them – it has scotomized bombing as terror from the air.[82] The history of pacification remains the peace movement's doppelganger.

81 In the bombing of German cities in the latter stages of the war, some 600,000 civilians burned, choked (firestorms sucked the oxygen from the air) or boiled to death. "Bomber" Harris referred to the blanket bombing as "Hamburgerisation". The bombing plan was drawn up by Air Marshal Portal, who in 1934 in Aden had assisted Air Marshal Trenchard, architect of the aerial bombardment of Mesopotamia. The imperial bombing line is direct from Iraq to Germany and back again.
82 A report (released October 28, 2004) in the British medical journal *The Lancet* calculates over 100,000 civilian deaths in Iraq since the start of the invasion (*not* including in Fallujah, site of

It is no part of our argument, however, that bombing campaigns always have the pacifying effects intended. Often they do, but sometimes not. The circumstances of the surrender of Japan may have led McNamara – like Rumsfeld after him in Iraq – to believe that the US air force could bomb the Vietnamese into submission. It was McNamara, too, who calculated the megatonnage necessary for the US nuclear arsenal by doubling (as a margin of error) the number that would ensure the annihilation of the Soviet Union, and then doubling it again just in case: here was the deep structure of the post-war peace – a version of terrorism dubbed "deterrence" (and sharing its etymological roots), based on a policy of bombing on a genocidal scale; in the limit case, threatening to repeat Hiroshima a thousandfold.

Yet neither atomic stockpiles nor militarized accounting could prevent the defeat of the US in Indochina. Nor does the present US war machine display much confidence about where the fifteen-year-long pulverization of Iraq has led it. Especially so because the bombing was premised on the assumption that the perpetrators could go on indefinitely making war from a distance, with no need to "fear vengeance in their homeland from the peoples whose homelands were their theatres of war".[83] The bombing of Manhattan, however, has threatened to change the terms of engagement.

The long history of imperial bombing, in other words, has now seen a new form of "blowback". The events that brought on the current crisis of the US state depended on the very technologies that underpinned US global hegemony and its "force projection" for over a half-century: the planes that struck the World Trade Center were in origin World War Two

---

some of the occupation's heaviest fighting). The estimates may go much higher, but what is most striking for our point here is that 95 percent of the civilian deaths were the result of aerial bombing.

83 Eberhard Spetzler, *Luftkrieg und Menschlichkeit, Die Völkerrechtliche Stellung der Zivilpersonen im Luftkrieg*, Göttingen 1956, quoted in Sven Lindqvist, *A History of Bombing*, p. 20.

bombers adapted in the 1960s for mass tourism and business travel, refunctioned by Atta and his crew as weapons of mass destruction. The components of this new anti-imperial resistance are, of course, manifold and complex. But whatever else this resistance believes and imagines, it knows well that imperial war is a permanent condition; it suffers no paralyzing illusions on the score of "peace".

Fundamental to pacification strategy is the fact that direct military intervention, and the devastation it brings, provides a smokescreen for the replacement of insufficiently cooperative local political cadres by (more or less) loyal "assets". The chaos, instability, and violent factionalism left in the wake of armed intervention lead to "creative tensions", to quote Donald Rumsfeld, within which the US can operate more easily and invisibly than with a normally functioning local state apparatus.

Further, the total militarization of territory permits permanent US emplacements, not only in the war zone but also in its periphery (known in military cant as "lily pads"). And with these bases comes a military bureaucracy that operates as a shadow government (with the help of compliant NGOs), primed to "advise" and "assist" the region's weak states. The Balkans and its new bases come to mind. Similarly, the US used its war on Afghanistan to establish or expand thirteen new bases across Central Asia. And the invasion of Iraq has resulted in the construction of new military installations in Qatar and Djibouti, plus major expansion of extant bases around the Gulf – all in addition to the "enduring camps" (fourteen by most recent count) that will remain long term in Iraq itself.

The chaos of ongoing war also provides camouflage for the implantation of external economic forces: the pumping up of an addictive regional arms trade, and the military and its contractors acting as advance men for "development" capital (e.g. pipelines, terminals, transport and communications systems), which gains a stranglehold on the weak states that emerge from the melee. In the longer term, warfare's devastation of infrastructure requires an infusion of handouts and investment with various neo-liberal conditions attached. In all of these ways, war's service to capital is to set the stage for the trinity of crude accumulation: the enclosure and looting of resources; the creation of a cheap and deracinated labor force; and the establishment of captive markets.

But even apart from these specific imperatives, modern imperial strategy seeks to impose dominant military presences in crucial regions *even without knowing exactly what or how well capital will do in the particular site of intervention.* That is because even if an intervention fails to bring about a coherent market structure in a given weak/failed state, the entrenchment there of the US military succeeds in the planting of a fulcrum for *future* regional maneuvering. For example, there is very little to interest American capital in Panama itself – the canal is no longer significant to a commercial world that maintains entirely separate ocean fleets. So, neither the US military's leveling of central Panama City during the deposing of Noriega, nor feeble efforts to rebuild it, have been of much moment to American corporate power. But the invasion did serve to reestablish US control over the Panamanian military, and to reenergize US military presence in Central America as a base for the future disciplining of the problematic South.

The Balkans provides another case. American intervention (piled on top of the civil war) so devastated Kosovo that more than five years later no one, except various mafias, is the least interested in its potential for development. But the American state still judges its campaign strategically successful – ignoring the false premise that the bombing "brought Milošević to the table" – because the US military now occupies the vacuum in the Balkans created by the Soviet collapse and withdrawal. Likewise, capital has little direct interest in Afghanistan. But – in addition to its role in the US response to the September attacks – the war there made possible extensive new American bases and inter-military connections throughout Central Asia.

Because of these broad, long-term phenomena, *it may not matter greatly* to the larger strategic project whether the invasion of Iraq results in a newly constituted coherent state open to market penetration under neo-liberal orders, or ends in a chaos of factionalized, fratricidal zones of brutal and shifting tribal or sectarian control. That is because a few key areas of even a partitioned, permanent state-of-siege Iraq might still be encapsulated for the exercise of Western capital – Basra, Rumaila, and the southern oil fields; Mosul and northern Kurdish (also oil) regions. More essentially, the war will have succeeded strategically *to the extent it has facilitated a significantly greater permanent US military presence in Iraq and much else of the Middle East* (including the desired subtraction of Saudi Arabia from the equation), positioned there for the next phase of imperial projection.

Of course, there may be serious consequences for the American state if the so-called restructuring process abjectly fails in most of Iraq. A failed state may provide fertile ground for the growth of still more unpredictable resistance in the region. And the degeneration of Iraq into protracted civil war, into a Shi'ite theocracy, or into mini-fiefdoms beyond central governance, may yet prove a real defeat – a defeat with strategic consequences – in the American state's struggle to reestablish plausibility on the terrain of spectacle.

Permanent war, finally, seeks always to *normalize* itself, and in the process to relativize the notion of "peace". Expansionist military interventions, if embarked on regularly enough, serve to maintain the image of war as an unexceptional part of the state's external political life. Weak citizenship is crucial to maintenance of social control, but even weak citizens must be inured to the extraordinary phenomenon of planes, missiles, and soldiers slaughtering people – and getting killed in their turn – around the globe. In order for domestic and "coalition" populations to consume war passively, they must have its (sanitized) images fed them in a constant stream. Concomitantly, frequent war keeps the liberal mind satisfied with, and mostly unquestioning of, the cruel peace. Even those who go into the streets when outright war is under way find it much more difficult – and we include ourselves in the company – to muster similar emotional energy in the face, for example, of the slow death from disease and malnutrition of hundreds of thousands of Iraqis under "sanctions".

Regular eruptions of war also stoke a culture of terror. The stifling and repression of domestic opposition – the direct terrorizing of citizens – is rationalized in the name of (homeland) security, patriotism, support for the troops. At the same time, frequent war is a way of rendering visible, through images of bloodshed – the indirect terrorizing of citizens – the "threat" against the nation which, because of its falsity, cannot otherwise be shown. (As these lines are written in San Francisco, the Blue Angels fighter planes are roaring and booming only a few feet overhead, with many in the crowd on the ground cringing, then laughing nervously, and finally nodding casually at "just entertainment". The same planes over Gaza City reveal their true business.)

VI

What we have been describing is the relentless structural energy that keeps the empire forever poised and leaning towards war. Our argument is that without recognizing this ever-present (im)balance of forces, it is never possible to comprehend how the vast war machine has come to be set in motion once again. Implicit in this argument is a rejection of the explanatory capacity of any lone gunman theory of military intervention – oil, Likud, Bush family vengeance, etc. However, we certainly do not dismiss such contingencies. The empire's strategic apparatus may always be teetering in the direction of military intervention, but its levers must still be pulled. And that is where contingency comes into play – a Hydra of greed, hubris, mania, and bureaucracy. Iraq is a case in point.

We have argued previously that spectacular defeat was one precipitating factor in the Iraqi case, intermeshing with a new set of imperial ambitions and the hungers of specific sectors of capital. But there are also the banalities of the state's inner life. There is always, need we say it, an almost constant drumbeat for war from the Pentagon: military careers to be made; an unending stream of ludicrously expensive weapons systems (new nuclear weapons; further failed prototypes of missile defense; satellite-guided drones) to keep on-line; and the bottomless Pentagon procurement/production/disbursement appetite to feed. And increasingly, wars – more so than sanctions, coups, and the various forms of corruption – funnel massive profits to those sectors of corporate capital best represented in the state apparatus. The details of the exponential expansion, and privatization, of military expenditure, and the Pentagon/Washington/corporate revolving door, have been thoroughly aired by others. Suffice it to say that this set of crude economic imperatives has reached unprecedented levels in the post-Cold War era, so that what we describe as "military neo-liberalism" – the true globalization of our time – has replaced and outstripped the military Keynesianism of a previous age.

As many have noted in the context of Iraq, ideological contingencies must also be accounted for: zealots of various stripes frequently gain the ear of the state. These range from the particular (Zionists in the White House and Pentagon, obsessed by the task of removing Saddam) to the generically imperial (the "demonstration effect") to the imperiously sociopathic ("Every ten years or so, the US needs to pick up some crappy little country and throw it against the wall, just to show the world we mean business" – Michael Ledeen, holder of the "Freedom Chair" at the American Enterprise Institute[84]).

---

84 Quoted in *Harper's*, June 2003, p. 11.

Shifts in international power relations may also play a role. The post-Cold War need to restructure NATO – to push its field of operations eastward, and to reassert US control over it – led to US engagement in Kosovo. The desire to rid the UN of any authority over war-making, and to substitute the judgment of the apocryphal "international community", was certainly part of the US push to invade Iraq. And some have argued persuasively that US concern over a battle between the dollar and the euro, particularly as the currency of oil, was a factor in the drive to Baghdad.

Finally, like most other self-respecting internationalists, we have always been inclined to dismiss the notion that domestic politics can drive imperial decision-making. We still reject "drive", but it is clear that domestic considerations do indeed play a role in the launching of military interventions: war in Kosovo was certainly intended, in part, to "upgrade" Bill Clinton's image as a leader; both Bushes seem to have hoped that war would distract the citizenry from economic troubles at home; Korea was in large measure a response to American capital's late 1940s domestic crises; and even the classic Monroe Doctrine was crafted in part to help John Quincy Adams – then Secretary of State and author of the Doctrine speech – in his upcoming presidential bid. Moreover, since the Reagan era, enormous military expenditures justified by threat to the homeland have provided cover for massive deficit spending by self-defined fiscal conservatives. When combined with radical tax cuts for the corporate and individual wealthy, this deficit spending has permitted the American state to plead poverty as it dismantles the social-democratic contract forged in the 1930s.

These, then, are the primary contingencies. One of them pushing in the direction of a particular military action is almost always insufficient on its own. However, when several such contingencies align, the preexisting structural inclination toward war may set off military intervention *regardless of the likely tactical efficacy of the particular action* – that is, even if the chances are slim of achieving any definable political goal. Further, once critical momentum toward military aggression is reached, the intervention is likely to begin *even though the various constituents cannot agree on why*. Regarding Iraq, it is now clear that when it embarked on its invasion, the US had no sense of whether its market-happy post-war reconstruction "plan" had any real chance of success. And the various elements and factions pushing for the war were so fragmented, even contradictory, that by their own admission they were forced to come up with a consensus rationale for the start of the invasion – weapons of mass destruction – which *none* of them actually believed.

VII

The invasion of Iraq has seen the state scrambling to keep its rationales for war one step ahead of the polite, self-policed queries of the media. So far, the spectacular enormity of the September 11 events has permitted the propaganda machine to maintain the necessary proportionality. That is, the plausibility required of any domestic ideological cover for a military incursion is directly proportional to the scope of the intervention and inversely proportional to public perception of the "evil" being addressed. So, even the most ludicrous invention – protecting American medical students from the depredations of proto-Communists – was sufficient to excuse the exceedingly brief and bloodless (American blood) invasion of Grenada. And the attack on the Taliban could be legitimized as part of a general War on Terror because the Twin Towers event was still recent and emotionally raw.

The war on Iraq may turn out to be different. Regardless of its shifting, counterfeit details – weapons of mass destruction one day, links to al-Qaida the next – it has been the notion of a direct threat to the American people that has had the most staying power. The "threat" motif has a long history, of course, and reactivates Cold War reflexes. And indeed there was a real attack on September 11, which still angers and frightens. But as the bodies and bills from Iraq keep mounting, and as the insurgency shows no sign of abating, the amalgam of threat rationales for the new war and occupation may well begin to lose their proportional grip. (We suspect that not a few of the Washington directors of the occupation privately hope for a steady diet of reinvigorating terror attacks beyond Iraq itself.) The US propaganda machine now frequently slips into its "humanitarian intervention/implanting democracy" mode, with this new legitimization of the occupation meant implicitly to revise the reasons for the war itself. This tactic too has a long imperial history. But it has gained new momentum in the last decade or so.

One of our abiding concerns about the state's return to such rationales for military incursion is the extent to which segments of the Left are willing to accept these propositions within a kind of "humanitarian internationalism", permitting human rights discourse to short-circuit their otherwise thoroughgoing distrust of the state. They have lost sight of the fact that in the hands of the imperial state, humanitarian intervention inevitably becomes "mercy by any means necessary", and in recent examples ends up following a monstrous logic of its own: the 1989–90 invasion of Panama left much of Panama City razed by bombing and 60–80,000 homeless; the Kosovo intervention unleashed a new round of ethnic retribution and resegregation and left the entire region ravaged and in the hands of various mafias; and the continued occupation of Afghanistan has led to the return to power of the warlords (with undiminished conditions of degradation and terror for women in most places outside of Kabul) and a return almost exclusively to an opium economy … "They make a desert and call it peace".

With regard to Iraq, in particular, the long-term domestic purchase of the humanitarian rationale already seems in jeopardy. Even on television the US public cannot help but see the difference between the man-on-the-street Iraqi and the slithering "leaders" – when rarely they are shown these days – hand-picked by the US to serve as brokers for the occupation. And the very racism that has helped feed an undiscriminating call for vengeance against Saddam–al-Qaida–Taliban–Arafat at the same time works to diminish public support for enormous outlays of bodies and cash for "ungrateful" Iraqi recipients of freedom.

In the end, however, the picture we have tried to paint in the preceding pages exceeds the question of justification altogether. For ultimately, as Hannah Arendt saw it in the chapter's epigraph, the endless accumulation of armed power proposes itself (or wishes to propose itself) *as the very basis of the social order*. This is the point of Arendt's invocation of Hobbes. "For if we could suppose", says Hobbes, "a great Multitude of men to consent in the observation of Justice, and other Lawes of Nature, without a common Power to keep them all in awe; we might as well suppose all Man-kind to do the same; and then there neither would be, nor need to be, any Civill Government, or Common-wealth at all; because there would be Peace without subjection".[85] For Hobbes, of course, the supposition was counterfactual. But because of this, no one has ever spoken more lucidly about the kind of sovereign he knew to be real (the kind we have been describing): "He hath the use of so much Power and Strength conferred on him, that by terror thereof, he is inabled to forme the wills of all .... And in him consisteth the Essence of the Common-wealth".[86]

By terror thereof. To forme the wills of all. And whoever calls this into question proposes an end to what we know of politics as such.

---

85 Thomas Hobbes, *Leviathan,* ed. C. B. Macpherson, Harmondsworth 1968 (first pub. 1651), p. 225.
86 Ibid., pp. 227–8.

4

THE FUTURE OF AN ILLUSION

An Eastern race well versed in Western culture and profoundly in sympathy with Western ideals will be established in the Orient. Furthermore, a Jewish state will inevitably fall under the control of American Jews who will work out, along Jewish lines, American ideals and American civilization.

—William Yale, US State Department consultant, 1919

Unrelenting mass resistance to its territorial occupations; a fraudulently "miraculous" economy wholly dependent on foreign subsidies; a grotesque legally enshrined apartheid; a political class in thrall to its military; a paranoid state-of-siege society; almost universal international opprobrium for the past two decades; and pan-Islamic resentment and rage fanning ever more violence against its lone apologist and protector. From the perspective of early twenty-first-century American imperial interests … a failed state. Yet despite this now unmistakable bankruptcy, US support for Israel's increasingly extreme version of the Zionist project remains unquestioned, unblinking.

We enter an analysis of the US–Israel relationship somewhat reluctantly, claiming no special insight into the realities of life on the ground for Palestinians and Israelis, nor into the convolutions of their internal politics. What we discuss here, we want to emphasize, is not

Israel itself but the US state's connection to it. We shall make no attempt to detail the brutality of the Israeli regime and the consequent immiseration of Palestinians; or the actual extent of the extraordinary overt and covert US support for Sharon and his predecessors; or the floundering of official Palestinian political structures. Many others, both inside and outside Palestine and Israel, are better equipped to do so than we are. And they have – comprehensively. Rather, what we grapple with here is the constellation of appearances and material conditions which has, within the United States, rendered that damning mass of information politically invisible. And which seemingly obliges the US to continue its unqualified support for the Israeli state, despite that support having become an enormous liability for the US's designs in the Islamic world.

Notwithstanding our reluctance, we believe we must break a long-standing silence on much of the Left concerning the actual genealogy – and precise dynamics – of the US–Israel relationship, and in particular the role of that relationship in the current imperial moment. We break the silence because we believe it impossible to grasp the sources and direction of recent, and future, US moves in the Middle East and Central Asia without reference to its failed Israeli client state.

Of course, the silence has not been total. Some voices on the Left have chosen to locate the US–Israel dyad entirely within the frame of the two cultures' shared anti-Arab racism. There are also conspiratorialists who see Israeli agents planted throughout the US political command structure, directing American state policy on precise instructions from Likud headquarters in Jerusalem. More commonly and insidiously, there is the uncritical acceptance of the US state's much-repeated assertion, now become a piety, that Israel is a crucial US "strategic asset". And across a broad Left political spectrum, apart from and often in the absence of any accompanying critique, there is passionate and abiding support for the Palestinian people.

The central inadequacy of these accounts and approaches, we believe, is their failure to bring into focus the nature of US imperial interests (and self-deceptions) in the case. No doubt it is true that anti-Arab racism has played a role in the construction of the US–Israel bond. Similarly, in recent years, ideologues with close relationships to Israeli political factions have reached positions of influence within the White House and Pentagon. But we thoroughly reject the notion – we have never seen it fashioned into a genuine argument – that such racism is a *causative* element in imperial policy, or that the client Israeli tail truly wags the US imperial dog. More significantly, we shall argue that the assertion that Israel is a strategic asset has always been at best a partial truth, and in recent years something close to a lie.

We propose instead that the core, the abiding silent animus, of the US relationship with Israel has been Israel's Middle East reflection of the pernicious double identity *of the American state*. On the one hand, Israel has been a play of motifs and appearances that for a period seemed capable of projecting a seductive image of capital onto the screen of the post-war world. It stood as the realization, in the most unlikely (but symbolically charged) corner of the earth, of a market-enriched, "democratic" future: McJerusalem, to sum the dream up in a word. And simultaneously, the Israeli state was emblematic of hyper-militarized, crudely colonizing Western power. The first aspect slowly grew to significance (more slowly than is usually assumed) as the imperatives of spectacular politics took hold within the post-1945 West; the second became increasingly prominent as the US empire became more deeply militarized – and spread its reach across more of the world – over roughly the same period.

In this two-faced role – *as exemplar of a society in which total militarization and spectacular modernity were fully compatible* – Israel has mirrored and mesmerized the American state for nearly four decades. But we believe that this exemplarity has been so thoroughly degraded in recent years –

Photo: Ricki Rosen/Corbis

International Security School, Shfayim Kibbutz, Israel, November 2001

indeed has been turned inside-out – that, in terms of US imperial interests, Israel as currently constituted has become an extreme liability.
Rather than working to erode or intimidate resistance to the implantation of American capital in the Middle East, Israel's intransigence now
furnishes that resistance with constant fuel. And rather than continuing
to offer a version of modernity to be embraced by the region's numerous
weak and vulnerable states, it now stands for a set of cultural and social
relations that is rejected by the forces of political Islam, in part *because*
those relations are equated with the entity "Israel". Every radical Islamic
website, every communiqué from Islamic militant factions, is filled with
denunciation of Israel and its American protector. As long as political
Islam can focus on the fact that modernity has taken *this particular form* in
its midst (however reasonably, however cynically, with whatever tincture
of racism-answering-racism), every effort of the US toward "soft"

penetration of the Middle East is doomed to fail. And all continuing US attempts at forced penetration – we have no doubt that such efforts will continue – will be met with the same broad-based, desperate resistance now confounding the American state in Iraq.

Unqualified US support for Israel, then, has turned out to be a geopolitical trap. (Even Tony Blair is capable of recognizing this.) Yet that support is unwavering. We shall try to parse some of the reasons for this, though we offer no simple diagram of causes. Every empire enters into commitments and implantations that it later regrets. (Blair can be unctuously regretful on the subject of Israel because Northern Ireland is always on a British prime minister's mind.) Our arguments about US support for Israel – about an imperial power's fascination with an image of its own double nature, and about the ability of that image to entrap the power that sought to deploy it – are offered here preeminently as a lens through which the US invasion and occupation of Iraq might come to make more (misguided) sense. In this regard, our analysis of US–Israel relations might lead to two versions of a question we have not heard posed elsewhere in quite the same terms: Can the US move into Iraq be understood as a delusional attempt to repeat the one-time "success" of the Israeli lodestar? Or, put another way, did the Iraq invasion follow from the (conscious or unconscious) recognition, finally, that Israel's time as a projection of the West – as an illusion – has come to an end?

I

The reigning state and media narrative is that the United States and Israel have always been soulmates. Most Left critique of the relationship likewise takes as gospel (usually unstated) that US backing for Israel began with the birth of Zionism. But the historical record reveals something quite different – that the US's unreserved, overweening support for the

Israeli state has extremely shallow roots.[87] The first organized stirrings of Zionism in the late nineteenth and early twentieth centuries evoked barely a murmur of interest among the American political classes. US imperial sights were then still focused almost exclusively on the Western Hemisphere and the Pacific Rim. The Middle East, and Palestine in particular, were regarded as British and French turf. The US was not ready to challenge the Europeans' hegemony in the region, and in any case the old colonial powers seemed comfortably in control – the Ottoman Empire was disintegrating, Arab and Persian regimes were weak and compliant. Moreover, oil had not yet taken its central place on the world stage. Despite this relative lack of concern, the imperial planners in both the State Department and the corporate boardrooms did take a clear and consistent position on the Middle East, as a result of straightforward geopolitical calculus: avoid direct conflict over the far-flung Ottoman territory; and court the oil-producing kingdoms, do not aggravate them. Strategically, Zionism was nowhere.

What little early support Zionism did generate in the US was disjointed, contradictory, and ineffectual. Britain tried to goad America into backing the Zionist plan in Palestine by warning that if Britain and the US did not support it, the Zionists would turn to the Germans, where indeed the project had the Kaiser's attention. But Germany seemed of little moment to the US at that point, so the argument had no purchase. Domestically, the Democratic Party of the urban Northeast counted Zionist Jews among its members, but they were not particularly numerous or influential. And in the same Northeast cities, some elements of organized labor supported Zionism as a way to stem the tide

---

87 In his major work on the US–Israel relationship, Noam Chomsky asserted that US backing for Israel is thin and "will very likely erode if Israel comes to be seen as a threat rather than a support to the primary US interest in the Middle East region, which is to maintain control over its energy reserves and the flow of petrodollars" (*The Fateful Triangle*, Boston 1983, p. 22). Somewhat to the contrary, we will argue that US state support is thin but entrenched, and that, except perhaps for a brief period, it developed *despite* having always been more of a threat than a support to control over petro-flows.

of working-class Jewish immigration. These awkward bedfellows were joined in the Zionist sack – think of old-world beds in which separation boards permitted sleep without fear of touching – by a smattering of Christian evangelicals who supported Zionism as biblically ordained. None of this backing was well organized, and it was unable to muster even the semblance of a strategic argument in support of the Zionist project. At the very last minute in 1917, the US gave a faint nod of approval to the Balfour Declaration. Zionism may have slotted idiosyncratically into Woodrow Wilson's Scriptural readings on "the people of the Book"; but he was finally willing to give informal backing to the idea of a Jewish homeland, despite opposition from his State Department, only because the consequences were to be Britain's problem, and the Declaration did not commit the US to any particular course of action in what was then a geopolitical backwater.

America's position toward Zionism during the inter-war years remained basically the same. There were no strong organized domestic political forces, either pro or con. Strategic analysis – as articulated by the State Department and the oil companies – argued *against* US support for a Jewish state in the midst of the Arab energy fields, but there seemed to be no urgency about it: the US was freshly cementing oil arrangements with the House of Saud, which promised a plentiful supply of oil and oil cash for the foreseeable future.

Everything was transfigured, of course, by the events of 1939–45. There was, first, the Final Solution, and emerging evidence of it. The story of political reaction to this catastrophe is complex (and most often shameful). But without doubt it was taken, by important sectors of the European and American public, to strengthen the case for the forced creation of a Jewish state, and not incidentally the end of the "Jewish question" in Europe. Whatever our verdict on this last contortion of European anti-Semitism – this last salving of European conscience, as usual at the expense of another Other – the upwelling of sympathy for Zionism was significant.

What needs to be emphasized here, however, is how little this pattern of events affected American policy during the immediate post-war years. Because another great transforming phenomenon of the war years was the rise to supervening importance of oil. What mattered to the US in the Middle East was the filthy black liquid, not the agonies of the diaspora in Europe. And this new obsession with petro-resources led the US *away* from support for then-gestating Israeli statehood. Since the 1930s, and with increasing insistence as the decade wore on, the Departments of State and War had argued consistently against US backing for a Jewish state in Palestine: the Middle East desk saw it as vital for the US not to be seen by Arab oil producers as responsible for the establishment of Israel; and the generals believed it was far simpler to maintain good military relations with feudal Arab regimes than to become the guarantor of Israel's security. Strategically, Zionism was seen, overwhelmingly, as a bad risk.

Two startling reminders here: On the eve of its birth, the political character of the new Jewish nation was still so protean, and its strategic posture still so much up for grabs, that it was the Soviet Union, not the US, which cast the first United Nations vote for Israeli statehood. Upon Israel's official recognition in 1948, the US imposed an arms embargo on the new state. As a consequence, the Israelis bought arms from the Czechs, with Stalin's blessing. The Cold War game was on. And the Israelis learned quickly how to exploit it. Their first successful connection with the US state apparatus was through the two nations' spy agencies. The Haganah (pre-Mossad Israeli intelligence) had deep, effective networks inside the Soviet Bloc – or, at least, successfully presented itself as such to the ever-gullible US spy bureaucracy – and was willing to work unofficially with the OSS/CIA in exchange for that agency's quiet support for Israel within the US government.

Overt backing for Israel was still perceived as a strategic liability, however. The diplomats and defense chiefs were immoveable. The US was more and more inclined toward direct penetration of the Middle East, in proportion to the waning influence of Britain and France. Couched in Cold War terms ("containing" Soviet influence and local Communist leanings), the 1950s Eisenhower Doctrine intended that the influence of the old colonial powers would now cede to that of the US, and aimed, above all, at controlling emerging nationalism – notably the threat it presented to the region's oil oligarchies. But within this project, Israel was seen as irritant rather than ally, and during the 1956 Suez crisis it proved just how nettlesome it could be. Israel's secret deal with the British and French – specifically excluding the US – had Israel provoking war with Egypt as a pretext for the old colonials to reclaim the Canal. Rather than backing the plan once in motion, however (as Israel, Britain, and France had expected), the US responded by determining from then on to shunt the British and French to the margins of the Middle East picture, to manage relations with the oil producers as much as possible on its own, and to keep a wary eye on Israeli duplicity.[88]

II

None of this is meant to deny that Israel did indeed come to serve, for more than a decade, as a US strategic asset. In 1958, following the creation of the United Arab Republic in Egypt and Syria, the marines landed in Lebanon to protect the Lebanese and Jordanian states from nationalist uprisings. The landing was intended, at the same time, to send a message to nationalist movements in neighboring countries. This second aspect of the operation was decidedly less effective: in particular, the West's Hashemite protégé in Iraq, King Faisal, was assassinated later that year, and a republic proclaimed, ending British domination. However, the US was not prepared, either militarily or politically, to risk

---

88   However difficult it may be to imagine now, during the Suez crisis the US asked the United Nations to consider an embargo of all aid to Israel unless and until it pulled out of the Sinai.

outright invasion of Syria and Iraq, so the marines were withdrawn after only a few months. Lebanon and Jordan had been "stabilized", it was claimed – but this direct exercise of American power in the region had been an object lesson in unpredictability.

Throughout the 1960s and '70s, the US remained deeply concerned about the spread of Left nationalism and pan-Arabism in the region, but saw serious limits on further direct military intervention. The Cold War risks were grave. And the development of US techno-military prowess, and its control over the images of war, had not yet progressed to the point where invasions of sizable out-of-hemisphere nations could be managed without heavy American casualties, and consequent domestic dissent. Moreover, the project in Southeast Asia was already under way, and this fully consumed US "hot war" capabilities.

For a short time, at least, Israel solved the problem. When the Jordanian monarchy was again threatened by a coup in early 1967, the Israelis mobilized troops and threatened to invade: the Jordanian monarchy regained control. Israel successfully repeated the move in 1970, when Syria threatened Jordan. Also in 1967, and again in 1973, the Israelis made war on neighboring states in which Arab nationalism had taken hold: the devastating preemptive strikes served to cripple the opposing states' armed forces, and left the defeated regimes politically unstable. The threat of a pan-Arab alliance receded. The US reaction to Israel's wars was clear. It approved wholeheartedly of the consequences of the Israeli strategy, and no doubt appreciated the anti-Communist patina which Israel added, somewhat hurriedly, to its propaganda. At the same moment, Israel began its lesser – but nonetheless notable – strategic role as middleman for secret US military support to repressive regimes throughout the world.[89] Rewards were soon forthcoming: solid

---

89 The list is long, motley, and grisly, including Idi Amin, Mobutu, Bokassa, Haile Selassie, the Indonesian junta, and the military regimes in Chile and Guatemala – plus not only the Shah of Iran but also the post-Shah mullahs (in order to keep the Iran–Iraq war on the boil).

American diplomatic support (if initially more cautious and tempered than in recent decades); substantially increased military aid; and the ideological cloak in which Israel has been wrapped ever since – "our great strategic asset".

By the early 1980s, however, Israel's short-lived strategic effectiveness had come to an end. The US was beginning to understand – excruciatingly so with the Iranian revolution – that it was no longer secular Arab nationalism (with or without socialist coloring) that posed the real threat. Political Islam had moved into the nationalist void; and, rather than being intimidated by the Israeli military degradation of secular Arab states, the Islamists were emboldened by it. Israel's invasion and occupation of southern Lebanon, beginning in 1978 and reaching its pitiless apogee in 1982, was a bleak moment for pro-Western regimes in the region. It fuelled a growing pan-Islamic fury.[90] And the Islamists began to speak directly, in a language infinitely more violent than that of Nasser and Mosadeq, of the United States as an enemy coeval with Israel itself. Direct assault by Israel on any one of the remaining secular Arab polities now seemed too great a strategic risk: a further weakening of their rickety state structures might lead to complete dissolution – and to some new version of the Iranian mullahs. Even the open secret of the Israeli nuclear strike force, which for a while may have set an unspoken limit to any moves against crucial Western interests in the region, began to produce as many problems as it solved. Deterrents provoke counter-deterrents. First Khaddafy and Saddam, soon now Khomeini.

By the time the collapse of the Soviet Union again permitted the US to launch a major military intervention of its own in the Middle East (the 1990–91 Gulf War), the first Bush administration took extraordinary pains to ensure that Israel *not* be seen to participate, even in its

90 Israel itself contended that fighters came to Lebanon from across the Islamic world to counter the Israeli incursion.

own defense.[91] When it came to massive military intervention in the Islamic world, there were to be no more proxies. Least of all the Israeli "Defense Forces". Nonetheless, US support and apologetics for the Israeli state and its strangulation of the Palestinian people has remained undiminished. But if the strategic asset is dead and buried, then long live the … what?

III

Strategy is one thing, imagery another. At the same moment in the 1950s that Israel was so badly miscalculating US strategic posture in the Middle East – a miscalculation that led finally to the Suez fiasco – it was launching a hugely successful campaign to produce and control the *appearance* of Israel for Western consumption. It funded and organized a state propaganda machine dedicated to exporting images of Zionist modernity. These images were initially designed to bring private American and European funds into Israel as much as to court Western government support, but in the end this illusion would succeed in capturing the American state imagination. Two motifs in particular proved irresistible: "Making the Desert Bloom", and "The Only Democracy in the Middle East".

Let us take them in order. From its beginnings, one strand of Zionist dreaming had been the idea of a return to the land – an end to the age-old image of the Jew as petty tradesman on the move at the margins of social space, and the founding of a new culture of physical labor and direct productivity under the sun. This was an element of Zionism that appealed greatly to some parts of the Jewish Left, even among otherwise internationalist labor federations, in early twentieth-century and inter-war

---

91 The US not only publicly refused to use Israel as a major staging ground for the war but even heavily pressured Israel to refrain from returning missile fire at Iraq if attacked by the now-legendary Scuds.

Europe. These moderate socialist milieux were one source of immigration to Palestine/Israel both before 1939 and after 1945; and they contributed to the steady stream of young Americans and Europeans who went to witness the Israeli miracle in the 1950s and 1960s, spend a season on a *kibbutz*, and report back to their elders in praise of the new frontier.

"Making the Desert Bloom" was both an image and a reality, each with many facets. We have no wish to deny the idealism of most of the immigrants. The long history of the diaspora in Europe was filled with misery. And the extraordinary horror of Nazism was close, determinant for many. In the desert, history would begin again. But in the hands of the propagandists – and this is our subject, sadly – the rhetoric of "Making the Desert Bloom" could hardly have been more transparent, more insistent. It stood for the victory of a dynamic Western modernity over a slothful Eastern dark ages. The pastiche of image-elements assembled by the Israeli state apparatus was aimed directly at the postwar West: Israel was Occidental, it was anti-Communist, it was redoubtably "white"; it celebrated the marriage of technics with "democratic character", by means of which an individual, agro-industrial entrepreneurial spirit would transform – was transforming – a barren wasteland, peopled only by the occasional goatherd, into a spreading oasis of green hyper-production.[92] And indeed, they were beautiful (in a Socialist Realist sort of way), those rippling-muscled young *kibbutzim* in singlets and shorts – above all the *sabras*, who could claim "birth rights" in the land – working side-by-side, unmindful of the desert sun, to create a new world. All in such stark contrast (of course, mostly unspoken) to the dark, shiftless, neurasthenic Arab hiding away from honest toil in the casbah, under cover of the burnoose.

92 One aspect of these images-for-export was the "Plant a Tree in Israel" campaign, which fed the desert bloom fantasy while simultaneously training Westerners to the notion of sending money to Israel.

It did not matter that in fact the *kibbutzim* were mostly East European and North African (that is, neither Western nor "white", in other contexts); that many operated on collectivist principles (which eventually caused the *kibbutz* itself to disappear from the image-machine); that the desert was neither empty nor barren (sustainable agriculture having been practiced by Palestinian Arabs for over two millennia); that the supposed desert miracle was based on disastrous diversions of water which disrupted or destroyed traditional agriculture, and led in time to high-stakes hydropolitical struggles; or that the noble hands-on blooming was soon to be replaced by the usual techniques and displacements of agribusiness. The image was in place. And likewise its twin, "The Only Democracy". We presume we do not need to rehearse for our readers the foundations of dispossession and disenfranchisement on which *that* fiction was built.

Neither of these conceptions of Israel was without precedent in the earlier twentieth-century imagination.[93] Our epigraph from William Yale demonstrates as much. But Yale and his like had tended to sound the note in an old-world "bulwark of Western civilization" register, and their advice to the State Department had been ignored. No vital state interest appeared to be served. And the idea of America's image actually *benefiting* from being worked out in Palestine "along Jewish lines" – that is, from a secular, spectacular doubling in the form of Israel – was still too outlandish.

It was not until the 1950s, when the US's pre-war class battlegrounds began to empty into the suburban tract-world, that the Yale conception of Israel (suitably reformulated) came into its own. Exactly how this spectacular transference happened has still, as far as we know, to be explored empirically. *That* it happened is clear. And some of the components of the mirroring and bonding leap out from a first survey of the evidence. The congruence between the set of appearances exported

---

93 The notions were explicit in Zionism's foundational ideology: "There [in Palestine] we shall be a sector of the wall of Europe against Asia, we shall serve as the outpost of civilization against barbarism" (Theodor Herzl, *Der Judenstaat*, 1896).

from Israel and American capital's own developing consumerist self-image was fatally attractive. There, on the edge of the desert, was an entire nation of new developments, a suburban dreamscape – modernity in full bloom. Every aspect of the Israeli settlements was planned, every element fungible, every imagined family happy in its project of building and consuming the New. The old, industrial, class-divided urban world – indeed history itself [94] – had been jettisoned in favor of life at the frontier. The myths were mutually supportive: the Israeli "settling" of the desert and the post-war US shift to the suburbs both resonated with American frontier mythology, as did the Israeli "removal" of pre-modern dark-skinned recalcitrants. And Israel was a democracy ...

We believe that this attraction of the US for its Middle East reflection was already well established by the time, in the late 1960s, that Israel began actually to serve as a strategic ally. And when it did, attraction became infatuation. For a while, the frontier itself seemed to shift, and all Western Asia loomed into view. Israel would act not merely as an outpost but a stepping-stone. In it and by means of it, capital would gain its first foothold in a crucial, and seemingly vulnerable, strategic region. The Israeli example would prove contagious. Pluralism and "development" would triumph over stagnation and autocracy.

Modern states are often slower to fall prey to a set of spectacular illusions and compulsions than other sectors of the societies they govern. But there is a corollary to this. Once a state cathects to an image-cluster – once it *sees itself* in a spectacular mirror – it may be the very last social actor to let go of its object of desire, or to see how counterfactual (and counterproductive) a worn-out illusion can become. So, we shall argue, it has proved in this case.

---

94 With the exception of the Holocaust, particularly when useful to the Israeli state; see Tom Segev's powerful and painful analysis, *The Seventh Million*, New York 1993.

IV

States try to make use of the spectacles they fall in love with. No sooner had the appearance of Israel become a functioning part of the US imaginary than its agencies set to work projecting the image back to the Middle East, as the poster child of Western modernity. And to its own citizens, as the hero of various Cold War passion plays. Israel was the Western David holding off the Eastern Goliath, or the champion of free enterprise facing down Nasserite "totalitarianism". It was alternately (or simultaneously) Judeo-Christian *and* secular (that is, modern through and through), therefore the antetype of godless Communism or Oriental despotism or threatening theocracy. Apply as needed.

Then there was the question of Israel's belligerence, its ongoing actions in the Occupied Territories, and the dominance of its military over society at large. Again, our topic here is not the actual dynamics and instigation of that process, about which others have written unforgettably, but the nature of *the US state's attachment to (and deployment of) the spectacle of Israel permanently at war*. We believe, in a word, that the attachment was rooted in self-recognition – that Israel functioned most deeply as an image, and justification, of the US's own culture of endless arms build-up and the militarization of politics.

Lately, this bonding and doubling has centered on the issue of Israel and Terror. Both Israel and the US have made terrorist tactics the baseline of morality against which all government conduct is to be measured, and "security" the all-consuming obverse of "terrorism". Within such a framework – in the West Bank and Gaza, in Lebanon, in the Balkans, in Afghanistan, and (for over a decade) in Iraq – the distinction between civilian and military targets and casualties has been obliterated, collective punishment has become accepted practice, and grotesquely disproportionate response to acts of resistance has become the hallmark not only of the Israeli Defense Forces but also of

'Making the Desert Bloom', separation wall at Qalkilya, West Bank, December 2003

"America under siege". All resistance is terrorism. All state violence is self-defense.

Through its support for Israeli policies, the US began to test the limits of its *own* developing unilateralism. The more Israel became isolated internationally, the more intractable became its defense by the US. United Nations resolutions that could not be vetoed by its protector were ignored by Israel, with full US backing, and erased from the stage-managed reporting on such subjects in the American media. Israel's nuclear weapons are a threat to no one, and in any case do not exist. When the US successfully blocked international consequences for Israel's incursion into, and later occupation of, southern Lebanon, the Israelis embarked on their now well-known attempt at a Revolution in Occupation Affairs: the slaughters in refugee camps; the bulldozing of Palestinian villages and orchards; bombing of homes and helicopter assassinations committed with US weaponry; shooting of rock-throwing children, and a "security" wall appropriating broad swaths of land and imprisoning an entire population. All of it immune from international response. And, more and more, such Israeli actions provided a model for the US's own conduct, in its pursuit of absolute impunity on the world stage.

Finally, endlessly, there is "The Only Democracy in the Middle East".[95] We shall spare readers the full vicious circle of syllogisms. Resistance to Israel just *is* resistance to democratic pluralism. Such resistance is essentially pre-modern, reflective of societies *incapable* – because of the "Arab mind", in Israeli cultural discourse – of non-tribal, secular allegiance and rational choice. Israel is hated not as an apartheid state, then, or as an occupier, or as a brutal suppressor of those who dare to resist, but because it is "a democracy". Since September 11, the same tautology has served to silence the possibility of any domestic debate regarding the sources of the New York attackers' rage, and, by extension,

---

95 Apartheid South Africa, one might recall, was "The Only Democracy in Africa".

that of resisters anywhere to US hegemony. They hate us because they hate freedom. And millions of Americans, who have heard the same mantra so often on behalf of the Israelis, assent to it one more time.

V

Our argument has been that Israel's brief period as a true strategic asset now lies in the past. The same can be said, we believe, about its time in the sun of the spectacle. Images of spotless orange groves, of shining white settlements with suitable color settlers, of El Al jets and Tel Aviv high-rises, of happy families lounging at Dead Sea resorts – all these have vanished from the pages and screens of Western media. Every corner of Israel now seen around the world is contested space, every Israeli in some extreme of rage or mourning: Uzi-toting settlers denouncing Sharon's softness; smoke-filled streets strewn with twisted metal, ambulances wailing, passersby screaming for revenge; Arab-Israelis and Palestinians spread-eagled against walls by police, soldiers or civilians (the distinctions harder and harder to read). Image victory has turned into utter image defeat. Even scenes of "normal" Israeli life, when rarely they appear, have about them a sense of emergency and duress. People seem not to stroll but to scurry, teeth gritted, more chastened than comforted by the deployment everywhere of armed force. Beleaguered David morphs into wounded, flailing Goliath. "Making the Desert Bloom" gives way to nightly footage of bulldozers leveling Palestinian olive groves. The frontier of freedom is now marked by a separation wall, every slab of which speaks of imprisonment, exclusion. The very *map* of Israel – the tourniquet of settlements and fortified superhighways cutting off life-flows across the West Bank, the scatter of Palestinian Bantustans, the political economy of the arid and the irrigated, and the Fence itself, with its unmistakable message of Divide and Rule – is unshowable, unspeakable.

Failure is compounded by a Revolution in Image Affairs in the surrounding Arab world. People no longer depend on images tossed back at them from the West, or filtered through their own dismal state media. They have built themselves an alternative wisdom: al-Jazeera, al-Arabiya and their imitators; scores of Arab-language newspapers and journals; multiplying cyberspaces. The Israel portrayed by this new apparatus, safe to say, does the US no spectacular service. Orientalism talks back.

Even as colonizer and enforcer – the aspect of Israel's spectacular identity to which the American state is most deeply attached, we feel – Israel has lost its efficacy. Nearly forty years on, the Israeli state is no closer to an end-game in the Occupied Territories. The Palestinian people, its own failed official structures notwithstanding, has proved indomitable. And indominability, over time, cannot be disguised or dissembled. As enough rock-throwing boys confront enough Israeli tanks, eventually they are seen as … tanks against boys – and no amount of casuistry will keep the "security" gloss intact. As more and more anguished Palestinian families sit in the rubble of their homes after yet another attack by helicopter gunships, eventually they are seen and heard as … gunships against families – and no amount of "reliable information" about terrorists can alter the equation. None of this means to suggest that the bombings of civilians in Israel by Hamas, al-Aqsa, and others are in any way excusable in response. The tactic is execrable and futile. But if Israel-the-occupier is a model of anything now, it is a model of abject failure.

VI

Why, then, is there no sign, however slight, of the US beginning to prize itself apart from this ally-become-ball-and-chain? We offer no simple or definitive explanation here, but we suspect the answer is *superficial*; for oddly, sometimes the worst entanglements are contingent and skin deep. In part the answer is to be found within the mix of American domestic politics – every empire has a home life. But also in the nature of imperial systems – most empires have their Northern Irelands; their Algerias; their Ottoman Balkans; their Moldavia and Wallachia. And even these comparisons may be overpitched. Each was, after all, a true colonization, an attempt to maintain the hold of a nation-state over a contiguous territory. There is no such imperial compulsion at work in the Israeli case. Compulsion – or at least, irresistible determination – happens now at the level of spectacle. Which does not mean that the grip of causation is any less tight.

What, then, are the causes here? No doubt there is some combination of factors that can be rightly if imprecisely called "the Jewish lobby". We have no interest in entering the tawdry conversation, which all too easily slips into conspiracy theory and vaguely (if not grossly) anti-Semitic hypotheses, about just how strong such influences are, or how large their bank accounts. Suffice it to say that support for Israel within the US is extremely well designed and well organized. The efforts of the American-Israeli Public Affairs Committee (AIPAC), along with other connected groups, have been targeted with real ingenuity through the years, focusing on the management and intimidation (here "lobbying" is too weak a term) of individual members of Congress, and on influence with key White House and Pentagon staff. Conventional advocacy and PR have continued; but, as is true of American politics generally over the last decades, it is access and "consultancy" that have mattered most.

In recent years these efforts have been aided, grotesquely, by the emergence of evangelical Christians as a political force. As the evangelicals began to summon and recognize their strength in the 1980s, the state moved to harness their dispensationalist views[96] into active political support for US policy in Israel. It proved possible to get these good Christians sufficiently to overcome their own personal and organizational

96 For dispensationalists, the most crucial sign indicating the imminence of the Second Coming is the return of the Jews as a nation to the Holy Land.

anti-Semitism (in the confines of the fundamentalist mind, dispensation-alism and The Protocols of the Elders of Zion are not mutually exclusive) to forge working relationships with Israeli and Jewish-American organi-zations. One only need see a photo of buttoned-down, Southern Christian politico Tom DeLay standing with black-robed, black-bearded *Hasidim* at the Western Wall to get the Buñuelesque flavor of the alliance.

To the extent that our subject is the balance of "influence" in Washington, then we should also enter into the equation the absence of any countervailing power. Palestinians have a small and relatively recent diaspora in the United States, without long-standing political organiza-tion. And the notion of a broader "Arab lobby" in support of the Palestinian cause is a phantom: Arab states have never been willing to spend their limited political capital with the US on the Palestinians' prob-lems, and pan-Arab political organizing within the United States is even more spectral than in the Middle East.

We are heading fast, we realize, into the mere totting up of political sums. And to a certain extent that is the reality of the situation. For *even at the level of the spectacle* there remain no pressing or persuasive reasons for the US to go on looking into the Israeli mirror. Israel, it has been clear for some time now, is a classic instance of a failed state – a charac-teristic product of Cold War over-armament plus "free enterprise" decay. But its failure, from the US point of view, goes deeper than this. It is a *failed spectacle*, above all – the first and most glamorous such failure, we predict, of a great new round to come.

It remains obscure how the imperial master frees itself from an illu-sion it has cultivated and cherished for four decades. In the first instance, it is trapped by its own apparatus of PACs and fundraisers and agents of influence. In particular, the evangelicals are a sorcerer's apprentice, let loose in a holy war but without any magic words with which to rein them in. And neo-con jingoes are especially well represented in the current White House and Pentagon: any turn away from Israel would be, for them, a deplorable and enraging sign of weakness – evoking the satanic name of Vietnam, no less, which never stops echoing in their skulls.

But the state is trapped by something more. Something that prevents the US from changing course, even though that course is clearly self-defeating – there will be no end to anti-American jihad as long as the matter of Israel and Palestine remains "unresolved" – and could be reversed by the hegemon with little consequence to its grip on global power. There is something deeper at stake here, something particular to the alchemy of spectacle. Support for Israel has long ceased to be a simple motif in a government-run propaganda flow – one that can be turned off at the tap whenever the state deems it expedient. It has become a compulsion, beyond mere adjustments in strategic design. The US, in a word, is in thrall to the image of its body-double. It is trapped by the logic of its own image-co-dependency. The state believes in Israel the way the addict believes in the next fix.

In nearly four decades now, the US has developed no strategic plan for the Middle East which includes a viable, independent Palestine. Instead, it kept afloat the pathetic Arafat as an alibi for refusing to address the dispossession of the Palestinian people. Likewise, it has imagined no version of the region that does not revolve around the "only democracy in the Middle East". This ideological addiction, this pathology of empire, leads us back finally to questions we posed at the outset: Can the US move into Iraq be understood as a delusional attempt to create a *new* "only democracy in the Middle East"? Could part of the impetus be, at last, an implicit recognition – at some levels of imperial power – that the phantasm of Israel as projection of the West has come to an end?

Delusional, indeed. And some delusions of empire may be markers of its late-stage morbidity. But this is cold comfort. For the horror of the present situation lies in the fact that the price of this delusional system is paid every day by actual bodies, actual death and despair, in Ramallah and Gaza, in Fallujah and Sadr City. Exactly this has been one main theme of our book. The spectacle, we have been arguing, is not merely a realm of images: it is a social process – a complex of enforcements and exclusions – devoted to the suppression of social energies, with the imaging and distancing of those energies being only one (among many) of its techniques. The spectacle, that is to say, is deeply (constantly) a form of violence – a repeated action against real human possibilities, real (meaning flexible, useable, transformable) representations, real attempts at collectivity.

When a particular node of the spectacle enters into crisis, as we have been saying has happened to the spectacle "Israel", it is precisely the *violence* of this process that comes into view. Ultimately, the spectacle comes out of the barrel of a gun. State power informs and enforces it. Mostly that fact is hidden. The spectacle *is* that hiding. But in the end, when a spectacle agonizes, the guns reappear at every margin of the image-array.

5

REVOLUTIONARY ISLAM

How to initiate the revival of Islam? A vanguard must set out with this determination and then keep going, marching through the vast ocean of *jahiliya* [the state of ignorance preceding and surrounding Islam] which encompasses the entire world. During its course, this vanguard, while distancing itself, somewhat aloof from this all-encompassing *jahiliya*, should also retain contacts with it. The Muslims in this vanguard must know the landmarks and the sign-posts on the road to this goal … they ought to be aware of their position vis-à-vis this *jahiliya* which has struck its stakes throughout the earth. They must know when to cooperate with others and when to separate from them … what characteristics and qualities they should cultivate … I have written Signposts for this vanguard which I consider to be a waiting reality about to be realized.

—Sayyid Qutb, *Ma'alim fil-Tariq* [Signposts along the Road], 1964

The Caliphate. Coming soon to a country near you.

—*Hizb'ut Tahrir*, broadsheet, UK 1996

No assassin, no propagandist of the deed, has ever matched the impact of the aviators who struck the Twin Towers on September 11. The event signaled the arrival in the heartland of global capital of a new model vanguard. Islamism: the new International.

It was predictable that, in the immediate aftermath of September 11, the public airwaves would be filled, not with a debate about the role of America in the world or the conditions producing political Islam in its most militant forms, but with the tired Orientalist litany: Islamic terror and Islam's bloody borders, Muslim rage, the Green Peril, barbarians' hatred of freedom, and the new Crusades. We have witnessed a unilateral declaration of war by the Islamists, said one nullity in the US foreign-policy establishment.[97] In this Manichean world, Islam was not simply pre-modern, it was anti-modernity itself. Muslims were (at best) "a nuisance … and always were a nuisance".[98]

Doubtless there will be those for whom what follows merely adds to this Orientalist chronicle. We have opened our chapter, after all, with the voice of a new Islamic vanguard draped in the cloak of revolutionary excess, dreaming of the return of the Caliphate. We know full well the dangers of collocating at the outset Islam and violence, of conflating the Muslim, the Arab, and the Terrorist, and of substituting a wholly unrepresentative strand of contemporary religious orthodoxy for the complex and heterogeneous firmament of Muslim belief, practice, and political expression. But those who properly dismiss the notion of Islam as a "totalizing cultural system" – the belief, in other words, that Islam is unique among world religions in its capacity to infiltrate all aspects of the social and political life of its adherents – must still come to terms with the fact that in the attacks of September 11 the worst fears of the Islamophobes (and perhaps their own) seemed to be confirmed. Yet we remain convinced that, in the rush to expose the logic of imperial oil or the new American militarism, the Left has passed far too quickly over the

---

97 Daniel Pipes, *Militant Islam Reaches America*, New York 2003.
98 Ernest Gellner, cited in Aziz al-Azmeh, "Postmodern Obscurantism and the Muslim Question", *Socialist Register 2003*, p. 46.

Islamic constellation – its historic mutations, social forces, and political expressions. In this chapter we try to face squarely the emergence of a vanguardist Islam – and what it means for the Left – and to locate its genesis in relation to the real diversity, and the heterogeneous politics, enveloped by the global Muslim community.

If Samuel Huntington, Daniel Pipes, and the American Enterprise Institute seized on September 11 for their own purposes, putting the image to immediate use, the other end of the political spectrum seemed dazed, paralyzed even. Confusion compounded with revulsion seemed to produce a sort of schizophrenia. Was this a strike in the name of a modern anti-imperialism, or grounds for a "just war" adequate to the horrors inflicted upon slaughtered innocents? Was it a time for solidarity, even patriotism? Had it become unthinkable, suddenly, to point to the deep narcissism and selectivity of America's compassion for the victim – to mention Rwanda or the Palestinian *intifada* in the same breath as the horrors on TV? The Left did not know then, and still does not know, exactly who ordered the attacks on New York and Washington, but the pilots' actions – and the rhetoric that followed – were nevertheless instantly recognizable as a form of *modern revolutionary politics*: they were precision strikes aimed at the heart of the American empire. Bin Laden himself declared that a blow had been struck by almighty Allah against the "vital organs of America"; the "real targets", he said, were "America's icons of military and economic power". It was not St. Peter's in Rome that was attacked, noted Olivier Roy; "it was not even the Wailing Wall. It was Wall Street".[99] For those who had spent the 1990s struggling against the IMF–Treasury nexus and its neo–liberal shock troops, could this be a case of "the enemy of my enemy"? But who could endorse the reckless destruction of the mammoth Buddhas at Bamiyan, the anti-Semitism of the Islamist vanguard, the banning of music and kite-flying, the grotesque

99 Olivier Roy, *Globalised Islam,* New York 2004, p. 46.

misogyny of the jihadists, and the very idea of democratic equality as unilateral submission before God? What cosmopolitan Leftist wanted *that*?

We know it will be argued by some that our account of Islamic politics grants revolutionary Islam – whether as a strategy of national liberation or as global Salafism – far too much weight. The militant vanguardism offered by al-Qaida and its network affiliates is, on this view, the handiwork of a tiny minority at the extreme edge of the Muslim universe. Their ultimate project is to retreat into the privacy of the mosque and the family: radical Islam in this account is "a trail of decline", its ideology "diluted" by the global economy.[100] The attacks of September 11, it is proposed, mark the death throes of a Muslim terror network that has neither legitimacy nor popular appeal … nor staying power.

This view strikes us as optimistic – and not simply because the US Institute of Peace places 0.02 percent of the Muslim world in the unacceptable "radical" fringe (that would be 300,000), or because more than 100,000 militants received military training in Afghanistan alone – and strangely out of touch with the political forcing house of "globalized Islam". The importance we attach to the very idea of a militant vanguard as a key symptom of modernity we shall return to in our final chapter. For the moment we simply wish to take note of a polling statistic: al-Qaida's political program – no Muslim, after all, turns to bin Laden for theological instruction or exegetical insight – sits comfortably with more or less half of all Saudis, Pakistanis, and Jordanians.[101] Richard Clarke asserted that there might be anywhere from eighteen to forty thousand Islamic insurgents operating under the al-Qaida banner. But there are, says Clarke – and we fully concur – "millions" of Muslims who occupy

---

100 Gilles Kepel, *Jihad: The Trial of Political Islam*, Cambridge MA 2002, p. 371.; see also Olivier Roy, *The Failure of Political Islam*, Cambridge MA 1994.

101 A poll conducted among 15,000 Saudis determined that only 3 percent support Bin Laden "as a leader" but 48 percent supported his political rhetoric (see www.igc.org, "Saudi Arabia Backgrounder: Who are the Islamists?", *Middle East Report*, no. 31, International Crisis Group, Brussels, September 2004).

a broad political ground largely indistinguishable from that occupied by the theoreticians of radical Islam, for example Ayman al-Zawahiri or Sayyid Qutb. This is not, we repeat, to lay a blanket of Terror over the whole Muslim *umma*. It is rather to acknowledge that large numbers of believers have come to see Islam in its *political* form – there has been a global discursive shift around exactly this question – as providing the only alternative to the actually existing authoritarianism of the Qu'ran Belt, where oppression comes mostly in *secularist* dress.

The task we set ourselves here is not to discuss the tactics of a Muslim vanguard, or to offer a full accounting of the motives of suicidal terrorists. Rather we pose the question: Why has a global neo-liberal order, organized in the service of secular American empire, provoked this particular, powerful form of resistance – ruthless, tyrannical and single- minded – and what is its relation to modern Islam? The attacks on New York, Bali, Istanbul, Casablanca, Nairobi, and Madrid were all made in the name of Islam as a political project. They were carried out by educated moderns whose reference points were not the traditional *ulama* or Sufi *tariqas*[102] but the Iranian revolution, the new *jahiliya* of the modern Brotherhoods, and the ideas of political theorists such as Sayyid Qutb (1906–66), Hasan al-Banna (1906–49), Sayyid Abdu'Ala Maududi (1903–79), Ali Shariati (1900–77), and Ismet Ozel (b. 1944). These were twentieth-century intellectuals, familiar with the ideas of Aristotle, Marx, and Nietzsche. In their writings (radically conservative, vitalist, and chiliastic) can be heard the echoes of the radical Romantics, of Herder, Morozov, Heinzen, and Schmitt.[103] They shared an abiding belief that the Islamic project had been left incomplete; and that its fulfillment demanded political *restoration*. Not, take note, a simple (and inevitably make-believe) duplication of the original Caliphate, but rather the creation of the *nizam Islami* – an Islamic order

---

102 *Ulama*: learned men, the guardians of legal and religious traditions. *Tariqas*: paths of mystical
     and spiritual enlightenment – which take various organizational forms within Muslim society.
103 See Aziz al-Azmeh, *Islam and Modernities*, London 1996.

with modern resonance. Central to modern Islamism is the desire – quite unlike the theory of government during the classical age of Islam – to hold the state as an agent of responsibility (in the face of any deviations of the existing Muslim community from Islamic principles) and as an instrument of salvation.[104] This modern Muslim intelligentsia spoke of a "new praxis", whose recruits in their student days often identified with Third World-centered *Marxisant* radicalism. Two or three decades later they sought to "Islamize modernity".

We devote attention to Islam because modernity's own account of the course of history – the song it sang to itself about the triumph of secularism in the modern world – has proved to be fatally premature. The opiates of evangelical Christianity, Hinduism, and resurgent Islam are the drugs of choice among the world's laboring poor. But it is only Islam – for now, at least – that can claim to provide a political project that is global in reach and ambition, anti-imperialist and (in some of its expressions) revolutionary in practice. That the attacks, and the subsequent acrobatics of theological self-justification by the insurgent Islamists, represent a perversion of Islam is surely true, but irrelevant for our purposes. The Twin Towers militants self-identified as jihadists; their murderous and psychotic impulses cannot obliterate this fact.[105]

Until such time as an insurgent rainbow coalition of Nigerian, Brazilian, and Korean Pentecostalists launch a vanguard insurgency against the heart of American capital, it is with Islam, and political projects made in its name, that we must come to terms. The universalism of its ideology, combined with its variegated yet disciplined organization, and the fact that it has so successfully seized the mantle of political legitimacy from the soured dreams of development, make the task of analysis

---

104 See e.g., Laura Guazzone (ed.), *The Islamist Dilemma*, Reading 1995.
105 Neither does the fact that George W. Bush sees liberty as "the plan of heaven for humanity" or that Jerry Falwell's spine-chilling fundamentalist response to September 11 was equal to that of any al-Qaida operative.

unavoidable. Political Islam has fed on the twin crises of (failed) secular nationalism and the (failed) post-colonial state. Its revolutionary face has been spectacularly successful; by which we mean not only the image-victory of September (leaving the US economy a trillion dollars in the red and a number of corporations, facing bankruptcy), but also the movement's success in capitalizing on the victory's aftermath. After three years of Bush's War on Terror, says the London-based Institute for Strategic Studies, al-Qaida now stands "fully constituted". It appears to have transformed itself from a vanguard organization into something like a mass movement with a nearly unlimited pool of potential operatives.

How is it, then, that so many Muslims have come to think politically with their religion, and what do we mean when we speak of the politics of Islam? We shall first provide a working definition of modern political Islam or Islamism – we use the terms interchangeably – situating it within a larger historical canvas. We then sketch the various currents of modern Islamism in order to understand the forms of revolutionary Islam and the wellsprings of its political energies.

I

> Every religion is in reality a multiplicity of distinct and contradic-
> tory religions.
>
> —Antonio Gramsci, *The Prison Notebooks*, 1952

All religions are in the business of propagating their basic ideas across the social field of which they are a part. Governing political classes, in turn, make use of dominant religious ideologies and institutions to legitimate their privilege and power. And to this extent religion – or, to follow Gramsci, one iteration of it within a multiplicity – serves a hegemonic purpose: what Bruce Lincoln calls "the religion of the status quo".[106] Hegemony of the dominant religion is always incomplete, and within its own ideological orbit (within Islam or Confucianism or Catholicism) there will always be other "distinct and contradictory religions" – "religions of resistance", in Lincoln's terms. There is no unity in their form — they may be militant or pacifist, utopian or nihilist, populist or despotic, ascetic or orgiastic – but they are all defined negatively, by their opposition to the religious status quo (one thinks of Jains, Taoists, Huguenots, and Vodun). For such religions to take on a *revolutionary* role, they must launch a political challenge to the legitimacy of the religious orthodoxy; they must broaden their social appeal and membership; and to do so, they come to depend upon a set of material circumstances in which a profound sense of crisis – a declensionist rhetoric is its hallmark – can be plausibly asserted.

We should not be surprised, then, by the long history linking politics and Muslim identity (any more than by the claim that Judaism and Christianity began as political movements). The Prophet was both the recipient of the Qu'ranic revelation and the founder of the first political community in Islamic history. The realization of God's will on earth is the prototype for all Muslim communities, the ideal in whose shadow Islamic jurisprudence, ethics, and political theory all developed.[107] Contemporary Islamic political movements are modern, wide-ranging and diverse: some emphasize preaching (*da'wa*) and social organization from below, some opt for flight and separation, some the ballot box, and others armed insurgency. But they are broadly unified by their advocacy of a political order which makes possible the application of the *shari'a* (Islamic law). They are part of a worldwide Islamic resurgence, and at the same time represent a radical challenge to an Islam of the status quo – embracing, it must be emphasized, a vast plurality of political forms, ideologies, tactics, and strategies. Islamism

106 Bruce Lincoln, *Holy Terrors: Thinking about Religion after September 11*, Chicago 2003, p. 79.
107 Malise Ruthven, *The Fury of God*, London 2003.

is rooted in the fact that millions of Muslims have been exposed to modern religious ideas outside the confines of traditional Islamic institutions – the *madrassas*, the mystical orders, the ancient brotherhoods – and raised on a diet of reasoning and interpretation (*ijtihad*) rather than imitation (*taqlid*) and the adopted policies of the founding fathers of Islamic jurisprudence.

To take one illustration, it was *sawha* preachers like Abdallah al-Hamid in Saudi Arabia – modernists who combined a Wahhabist outlook on social issues with a contemporary Brotherhood orientation to politics, democracy, participation, and civil society – who came to dominate the so-called "rigid" Wahhabist landscape of the 1990s in the Gulf.[108] In parallel fashion, a public Muslim intellectual like the Syrian engineer Muhammed Shahrur,[109] whose book *al-Kitab wa-l-Qu'ran* has sold hundreds of thousands of copies across the Arab world, draws an analogy between Qu'ranic reasoning and the Copernican revolution. His ideas directly challenge the traditions of Qu'ranic exegesis and Islamic jurisprudence. What is at stake here – and across Islamdom – is the indisputable (if paradoxical) fact that radical Islamism instigates a *democratization* of the religion, opening up the status quo to a panoply of lay actors who can lay claim to the interpretation of key texts.[110] Political Islam draws its strength, then, from the collapse of hierarchical notions of religious authority based upon assertions to the unquestioned mastery of religious texts. Even in Muslim states where such Islamic authorities

---

108 Wahhabism is a term that has increasingly lost its analytical significance. It has become a synonym for austere, conservative Islam. But Wahhabis (who refer to themselves as *muwah-hidun*) embrace a vast array of religious and political dogmas, from jihadism to political reform to social reform to so-called *sahwa* 'rejectionism' to liberalism. Wahhabism is in any case not the only Muslim denomination in Saudi Arabia (the people of Hijaz, which contain the holy cities, do not even follow Hanbali law, on which Wahhabism is based). See www.igc.org, "Saudi Arabia Backgrounder", *Middle East Report*, no. 31, International Crisis Group, Brussels 2004, pp. 8–12.

109 Shahrur's ideas and the debate around them can be followed at http://islam21.org.

110 Here the reference is *ijtihad* – a legitimate means of reasoning within Islam that turns on interpretation, creativity, and imagination.

are state-appointed (and state-funded) – for example Saudi Arabia, Iran, Eqypt, Oman – the word of the status quo will not necessarily be heeded. The new movement's appeal is cross-class, typically male-dominated (democratization only goes so far[111]), and rooted in the discontent of the armies of new migrants and deracinated city poor crowding into the slum-barracks of Baghdad, Cairo, Casablanca, and Jakarta – as well as the ghettos of the north.

There is no doubt that Islamism is restorative in its impulses: it glances backward to life under the authority of the Prophet and the four successor Caliphs. But at the same time it deploys a distinctively twenty-first-century set of political technologies, ideas, and practices. This program is to be contrasted with the scripturalist or traditionalist (sometimes called 'neo-fundamentalist') movements such as the Taliban, who do indeed resemble a pure counter-modernity – reviled as medieval obscurantism by the Iranian *mullahs* across the border. (But even here caution is in order. The Taliban too exhibited a firm grasp of modern forms of spectacle, surveillance, and intimidation.) The ground of modern political Islam is still open, still evolving. Here are its contours sketched for us by a CIA man – a retired vice-chairman of the Agency's National Intelligence Council – not suffering from "intelligence failure":

Islamism represents the largest, and often the sole alternative to most entrenched authoritarian regimes today ... violent and peaceful, radical and moderate, ideological and practical .... a vehicle for numerous Muslim aspirations: a desire to restore Muslim dignity and voice in the world, to create a new Islamic identity, to remove present dictatorships, to achieve democracy and greater social justice, to restore a moral compass to Muslim society, to achieve greater power for the Muslim

111   There is of course a vital, expansive debate within Islamist circles over gender and the role of women in the public sphere. See the "Muslim Modernities" Workshop at University of California Santa Cruz: http://www2.ucsc.edu/cgirs/conferences/islam/modernities.html.

world, to reject foreign domination, and [to defend] the rights of oppressed Muslim minorities everywhere.[112]

We must begin from the fact that political Islam – and its revolutionary vanguard variant too – is a conspicuously modern phenomenon. But that exactly does *not* mean that there were no politics in Islamdom until the modern era. On the contrary, and as with all major religions, the history of Islam reveals movements of reform (*islah*) and reinterpretation (*ijtihad*), which have served as political and institutional forces across Islam's entire span.[113] Indeed they were central to the political successes of the classical age. But the triumphal progress of the Prophet's movement and the territorial conquests by his immediate successors (the 'rightly guided' Caliphs) were not sustained. The idea of an Islamic state, Islam's aspiration to universality, and the message of social justice and equality all quickly foundered, in the years following the Prophet's death, on the reefs of dynastic, sectarian, and tribal division. Civil war, the implosion of the Arab empire, the draining of Caliphal legitimacy, and deep political fragmentation – these were the factors that contributed to early Islam's failure at the level of government and state formation. In the absence of a church or priesthood, early Islamic political authority came to rest in two lay constituencies: a warrior caste of tribal leaders, for whom Islam served as a basis for social solidarity, and the *ulama* (the lay interpreters of the law), possessing no executive authority and reliant

---

112 Graham Fuller, *The Future of Political Islam*, London 2003, cited in Clifford Geertz, "Which Way to Mecca?", *New York Review of Books*, July 3, 2003, pp. 38–39.

113 Muslim believers all over the world insist that the *Qu'ran* is the literal word of God as revealed, over twenty-three years, to the Prophet Muhammad through the Angel Gabriel at the onset of the seventh century. Most of its verses were revealed in direct relation to material and social conditions then confronting the early community of believers. A number of "sciences" (for example *ijtihad* [legal or creative reasoning] which flourished in the ninth and nineteenth centuries) were developed to understand the reasons for, and preconditions of, specific verses, and to understand how in their specific meanings they could be made to speak – based on reason, deduction, and prioritization – to the historically changing circumstances in which a community of believers found itself.

on external sources of power. In pre-modern times, Islamic societies were held together by a complex mix of clan, family, and mystical Sufi brotherhoods.

The Islamic state, then, was never able to rise above the essentially local (so-called "tribal") matrix, appearing as a conspicuous disappointment in the social imaginary of normative Islam's early success. Early triumphalism was further compromised as the Islamic world came under Western colonial domination. As a result, modernization within Islamdom proceeded along a secular path while religion remained in the custody of the *ulama*. Islam never bonded with the state in the way of Christianity (in Protestant Christianity the struggle occurred within the churches and teaching institutions, while in Sunni Islam it was driven by secular elites who wished to integrate politics along Islamic lines). An incomplete "Reformation" – we reserve judgment on whether contemporary radical Islam has affinities with the Puritan saints who helped pave the way for Lockean liberalism – has long remained a source of weakness. It was left to political Islam to turn the weakness into a strength.

That took time. Over the *longue durée* of politics within Islam, a distinction is customarily made between the "reformists", offering to renovate from within the traditional ranks of the *ulama*, and "modernists" challenging their monopoly of interpretation. In practice the traffic in ideas between them has been brisk. The origins of Islamic modernism, or what one might call modern reformism, lie deep within the historical record, as a reaction to seventeenth-century European imperialisms and Hindu–Muslim syncretisms. But it is within the force field of late-nineteenth-century European empire and early-twentieth-century Ottoman collapse that a distinctively modernist movement comes into being, offering the vision of a modern Islamic state capable of both reviving and refiguring the Caliphate. The ideas of Sayyid Ahmd Kahn (1817–98), Jamal al-Din al-Afgani (1839–97), and Muhammed 'Abduh (1849–1905) were crucial. The modernists' watchword was *salaf* – harking back to the pious "predecessors" of Islam's inaugural generations. The Salafists despised the inertia of latter-day Sufism and its cult of the saints, railed against Sufi corruption, and denounced the collusion of the Muslim clerisy with empire. In place of the present, they dreamt of a Muslim world united across the Sunni–Shi'ite divide and within Sunni Islam across the four legal schools or rites. After the First World War, the Salafiyya movement[114] aligned itself with a resurgent Wahhabism in the new Kingdom of Saudi Arabia but its focus was largely religious reform even if a more political wing contributed, in the 1930s and 1940s, to the nationalist movements in Morocco and Algeria. But already they were confident that the great inheritance of Islamic science and technology could be revitalized by selective use of what the West had to offer in the same fields.

Islamic modernism, in other words, was complex and ambitious. But, politically and strategically, it proved unable to mobilize Muslim civil society. It was not until the 1920s and 1930s, and then primarily as an offshoot of a series of pietistic, proto-fascist youth and sporting movements, that a series of innovations finally began to supply the political and organizational framework of the radical Islam we know.[115] Perhaps the formative movement in which Islam and modern political organization were linked – and one with filiations to the instigators of September 11 – was the Muslim Brotherhood (*Jam'iyyat al-Ikhwan al-Muslimin*), founded in 1928 by Hasan al-Banna,[116] an Egyptian schoolteacher who

---

114   The contemporary Salafiyya movement is often taken to be identical to Wahhabism (in fact they are rather different) but it has actually reverted from its original political vision to a mainstream "scholarly" form (*Salafiyya 'ilkiyya*), largely apolitical and preoccupied with proper behavior. A distinctive militant wing of Salafiyya – so-called "warrior Salafiyya" – developed out of the Afghan campaigns and is linked to al-Qaida.

115   See Aziz al-Azmeh, *Socialist Register 2003*.

116   Al-Banna brought together the Salafist views of Rashid Rida (rejecting the stultifying interpretations of the official *ulama*) with the notion, taken from the Persian Shi'ite al-Afghani, of creating a modern Islam through positive social, political, and (if necessary) military praxis. Al-Banna explicitly rejected, however, the colonial conditions with which the Salafists were prepared to coexist.

took his reformed Islam into private mosques and schools to avoid state control. The Muslim Brotherhood was an association serving workers in the British-controlled Suez Canal Zone, which developed into an organization designed to Islamize civil society – schools, clubs, professional associations, social welfare services for the new city districts – in order to seize political power in the name of a modern Islamic state.[117] This is not the place to rehearse the details of the Brotherhood's innovative recruitment, its flexible organization techniques, its secret militias and cell structures, its crypto-communist bureaucratic discipline, or the internal splits and sectarian divisions in the Nasserite period. What matters is its urban, mass character, and the extent to which it irrevocably shifted Islamic governance from the *shaykhs* to the urban professionals, from the trustees of religious tradition to the Western modernizers. It was the idea of Islam as a parallel world within the crucible of the new modern city – a positive set of institutions, keeping the secular state at bay – that was to prove the key to the future.

During the 1950s and 1960s the Brotherhood, and other incipient forms of Islamism, were fueled by the first storm of post-war petroleum revenues, and especially by the militants' innovative dual strategy of capturing the public education system and vital professional associations. By the time of the oil boom proper in the 1970s, which underwrote a huge expansion of state education at all levels, the public schools had become the battlefield on which the *ulama*, the Islamists, and the state struggled for control. Arab nationalism was most often the new Islamism's sworn enemy, yet it was nationalism and secular state-building that proved to be the Achilles' heel of Middle East states. Islamists rooted their efforts in local forms of communalism. At moments their organizations seemed to be moving toward genuine

---

117 Here al-Banna broke with the Salafiyya: if they sought to "modernize Islam", his project was rather that of "Islamizing modernity". Al-Afghani argued that constitutional government was key to Muslim progress; al-Banna's rallying cry was "the *Qu'ran* is our constitution".

countrywide mobilization; at others they fragmented into harmless warring sects. It was from within this political vortex that revolutionary Islam emerged.

The central political figure in the annals of revolutionary Islam is Sayyid Qutb. Born to an educated family in Upper Egypt, he was trained in a Western-style academy, and began his career as a writer, publishing poetry and works of literary criticism while employed by the Ministry of Education. After becoming a member of the Muslim Brotherhood in the 1950s, Qutb forged a theory of the Muslim vanguard (*haraka*), drawing upon a wide range of sources – from al-Banna to the Pakistani jurist Maududi, from the European Romantics to the French Vichy collaborator and eugenicist Alexis Carrel. His revolutionary texts – *Signposts, Islam: the Religion of the Future*, and his thirty-volume magnum opus *In the Shade of the Qu'ran* – were in part drafted in prison, where Qutb was tortured and finally executed by the Nasser government in 1966. He wrote, in short, under conditions not too different from Gramsci's; but he turned out to be Islamism's Lenin.

Qutb provided the canonical texts for urban insurrection. But his frame of reference was neither Egypt nor national liberation, nor even specifically the Arab world, but rather a utopian, *universal* revolution. Qutb's two leading ideas were *jahiliya* – as applied to the present – and the establishment of *hakimiya* (divine sovereignty on earth). His interpretations of the *Qu'ran* and the *hadith* (prophetic traditions) added up to a real revolutionary program: Islamic opposition to state terror; equality and freedom as common submission before God; the *shari'a* as the sole source of sovereignty; the approbation of "physical science" but alongside it a radical disavowal of "philosophical" inquiry; a moral critique of post-Enlightenment political theory; a rejection of the liberal separation of church and state; and a formidable critique not simply of the spiritual bankruptcy of the West but of the entire landscape of liberal civilization. Modernity was "a gigantic lie". Marxism and capitalism were terminal states of moral exhaustion, and everything outside the "house of Islam" was a "house of war". The Egyptian state was condemned as an agent of this ignorance and depravity, and therefore to be opposed – "annihilated" was his term – by armed struggle.

Qutb's most influential disciple was Muhammed Abd al Salam Faraj (1954–82), head of the Jihad Organization (*Tanzim al-Jihad*) that assassinated Anwar al-Sadat. Here lay the immediate Qutbian legacy: a wave of revolutionary affiliates such as the Islamic Liberation Group, *Takfir wa'l Hijra*, the *Mukafaratiya* ("Denouncers of the Kafirs"), the *Jund Allah* ("God's Soldiers"), and the Islamic Group (*Al-Jama'a al-Islamiyya*), spun off from the outer perimeter of the Muslim Brotherhood, which transformed Egypt after 1974, and especially between 1992 and 1997. But Qutb's political message extends much further afield. The Qutbian program is immediately recognizable as the stock in trade of many contemporary Muslim militant groups: Islamic Jihad, al-Qaida, the Armed Islamic Group, the al-Aqsa Martyrs Brigades, the Great East Islamic Raiders Front, the Moroccan Combat Group, the Abu Sayyaf. Some target the "near enemy", and aspire to be movements of national liberation – for example, the *Mouvement Islamique Armé* or the *Mouvement pour un État Islamique* in Algeria, both of which seek the revolutionary establishment of an Islamic state. Others (al-Qaida is the paradigmatic case) are transnational in emphasis, fixated on the distant hegemon and a global *umma*: "we must move the battle" said al-Zawahiri, "to the enemy's grounds".[118] Some invoke jihad as an obligation incumbent upon every Muslim. The takfirists go further still, seeking to cleanse society at large, holding that failure to take up jihad is apostasy, punishable by death. All are Qutbist through and through.

---

118 Bin Laden's mentor, Dr. al-Zawahiri, first laid out al-Qaida's strategy of attacking the "faraway enemy" in his December 2001 manifesto *Knights under the Prophet's Banner* – a tract that paid homage to Qutb's "spark that enflamed the Islamic revolution against Islam's enemies throughout the world". See Ayman al-Zawahiri, "Knights under the Prophet's Banner", in Walter Laqueur (ed), *Voices of Terror*, New York 2004, p. 430.

Much could be said about Qutb's oeuvre – his poetry, his subtle and nuanced exegesis, and his utopian re-imagining of the whole Islamic project. Here we treat only his political rationale for a vanguardist Islam. It is part diagnosis, part prescription. The greatest threat to Islam, so he argued, is posed by liberalism – precisely because of that movement's ability to *sideline* religion, to separate it from the political sphere, and from life in general. The result is a devitalized materialism (is it any surprise that the leader of the Palestinian Islamic Jihad, assassinated in 1995, was a partisan of T. S. Eliot?). The defining moment of this history, in Qutb's view, had been the collapse of the Ottoman Empire in 1924 at the hands of Mustafa Kemal Ataturk. Ataturk had been the carrier of the virus of liberalism into Islam's heart. Let us recall that in bin Laden's famous post-September 11 video, he referred to "more than eighty years" of humiliation. This is a specifically Qutbist reference: the watershed is still Ataturk's submission to secular modernity, and his abolition of the Ottoman Caliphate.

Qutb's prescription called for more than just jihad: it demanded a tight-knit vanguard capable of combating the dangers of *jahiliya* and the prospect of Islam's extinction. By vanguard, Qutb meant a cell of reno- vators holding themselves aloof from the filth of *kufr* (disbelief), and capable of detonating both a global assault against all forms of *jahili* barbarism and of rebuilding an authentic Islamic society. It was Qutb's time in the United States, during the early 1950s, that catalyzed his shift from a defensive notion of jihad to an offensive vanguard, for whose members there was "no real loss in their death, since they continue to live". For Qutb, the US was a nightmare of racism and degeneracy. Upon his return, his sense of the vanguard's task and tactics crystallized. "Purifying the filthy marsh of the world" was to be done by means of armed struggle, with acts of martyrdom an indispensable tactic. Four decades after Qutb's death, al-Qaida's chief "theoretician" Ayman al- Zawahiri, had developed "the method of martyrdom" into the "most

REVOLUTIONARY ISLAM   149

successful way of … burn[ing] the hands of those who ignite fire in our countries".[119]

Qutb's conceptual framework, despite his purported rejection of the West, drew on the rich history of both Muslim and Western thought. In many respects his narrative is instantly recognizable: the familiar dialectic of rationalization and Westernization, seeking to "abolish, transcend, preserve and transform modernity".[120] In the process of engaging with and assimilating modernist ideas, Qutb came to see Islam more and more in *aesthetic* terms: revelation was a divine art, and true Islam required an existential leap of faith – resting on the recognition that consciousness, not knowledge, is the ground for Being. (Nothing could be further from Qutbist argument than a "correct" – ahistorical – reading of primary texts. Qutb himself rejected traditional exegesis outright.) His was a radical agenda for the entire Sunni world – and indeed, a decade or so after his death, for the Shi'ite revolution in Iran. A straight revolutionary road connects Qutb to bin Laden's founding charter for al-Qaida: Sayyid Qutb's younger brother, Muhammed, fled to Saudi Arabia after his brother's death, and taught at King Abdul Aziz University. Among those who attended his lectures was bin Laden. And bin Laden's own some-time mentor – Abdullah Azzam – was a friend of the elder Qutb himself.

The creed of revolutionary Islam, then, is utterly hybrid. Its tactics and strategies borrow heavily from the Marxist canon: vanguardism, anti-imperialism, revolutionary terror, and popular justice. The political impulse behind the deployment of these ideas is, as we have seen, sometimes global, sometimes local, sometimes inward and separatist, sometimes outwardly assertive so as to "inflict the maximum casual-ties".[121] Often it is difficult to separate the two (al-Qaida, lest we forget,

119 Al-Zawahiri, "Knights under the Prophet's Banner", ibid., p. 430.
120 Elizabeth Euben, *Enemy in the Mirror*, Princeton 1999, p. 167.
121 Ayman al-Zawahiri, cited in Marc Sageman, *Understanding Terror Networks*, Philadelphia 2004, p. 23.

is the offspring of Saudi and Egyptian militant Islam, directed against a worldwide anti-Islamic conspiracy ["Zio-Crusaderism"] led, it believes, by secularists, Jews, and Shi'ites). There is no unified body of Islamist thought and practice, and this holds true *a fortiori* for its most militant forms of expression. Nowhere is this clearer than in the recent history of al-Qaida itself: ferocious disagreements among all manner of factions and cells, with ceaseless splitting and internecine strife (the sectarian history of recent North Atlantic revolutionary struggle looks tame by comparison). A map of insurgent Islam anywhere pushes political cartography to the limit. The Algerian Salafist and Brotherhood sects, for example, whose tactics defined the field of armed struggle through much of the 1980s, had morphed into at least nine different armed groups by the early 1990s, each crosscut by its own internal "tendencies" and networked affiliations to internationalist groups in Afghanistan, Pakistan, and the Gulf. The jihadi face of Saudi Wahhabism – customarily bundled together under the moniker "al-Qaida on the Arabian Peninsula" – is no less hybrid and sectarian. What they shared was a common modernity and internationalism. In Marc Sageman's inventory of nearly two hundred global Salafi *mujahidin* – recruited from the Maghreb, West Asia, the Caspian, and southeast Asia – almost three quarters were college graduates with a secular education, almost half were "professionals" and 70 percent had joined the jihad in a country in which they had not grown up.[122]

The common denominator, across these divides, is the fact that the Islamist intelligentsia was most often the product not of the religious schools but of universities with a curriculum (official or otherwise) centered on Marxism, Third Worldism, and the literature of national liberation struggle. These men took the playbook of Marx, says Olivier Roy, and injected it with Qu'ranic terminology.[123] The reach of political

---

122 Marc Sageman, *Understanding Terror Networks*, Philadelphia 2004, pp.70–96.
123 Olivier Roy, *Failure of Political Islam*, p. 3.

Islam extended well beyond the universities, of course; it was in the slums of West Asian and North African cities that Islamism seized the imagination of a broad swath of urban youth. It revived the project of anti-imperialism, couched now in the language of community decay, state illegitimacy, and moral bankruptcy. As we write in late 2004, the vast majority of Muqtada al-Sadr's Mahdi Army is drawn from this urban underclass, from the sewage-strewn slums of al-Hayaniyeh in Basra and al-Hurriyeh in Baghdad. It is a signal achievement of the US occupation of Iraq that by the spring of 2004 it had succeeded in uniting the Sadrist Shi'ites and the radical Sunni Salafists in a single, loose-knit insurgency.

II

More than once thus far we have stressed how the various strands of political Islam fed on ideas imported from the West. Nowhere was the involvement deeper – and more damaging – than in Islamism's framing of the idea of revolution, when it came to entertain it, around the twinned notions of vanguard and violence. It is *the thinking of each concept strictly and exclusively in terms of the other* that is the essential inheritance. And both are transfigured – here too the debt to nineteenth- and twentieth-century revolutionary tradition is fundamental – by an ethic (a metaphysics) of ascesis, mercilessness, and redemption. "Jihad and the rifle alone", "History does not write its lines except in blood": the phrases issue from the mouth of Osama bin Laden's early mentor Sheik Abdullah Azaam, but their attitude to agency and temporality comes to us directly from St. Petersburg and Zurich.[124] Politically speaking, Hezbollah and the Moroccan Islamic Combat Group are faithful imitations of the European counter-Enlightenment. The names of the Islamists groups are most often, as al-Azmeh reminds us, echoes of

124 See www.religiscope.com.

those adopted by ascendant modern nationalisms – Renaissance, Salvation, Awakening.[125] The apocalyptic romanticism, the myth of Armageddon, the post-Kantian aesthetics, the figure of the political martyr – all of these are born again in the beliefs of what bin Laden calls the "blessed group of vanguard Muslims".

There is nothing new, in other words, in the tactics and self-understanding of Islam in its revolutionary form. And yet the new vanguard has been able to take advantage of the new world order in ways that have left most other forms of opposition far behind. The question must be how.

Let us start from the fact that Muhammad Atta's final message to his eighteen militants was delivered by e-mail: "The semester begins in three more weeks". Both medium and message are significant here. Once entrenched in Afghanistan in the late 1990s, al-Qaida managed its international operations with ever-increasing electronic sophistication and audacity. Directives were encrypted in a quaint corporate language – terror was "commercial activity", bin Laden was dubbed the "contractor", the Taliban became the "Omar Brothers Company" – but at the same time made use of the Allied Forces' cryptographic system used in World War Two. Al-Qaida, that is to say, was from the start a modern virtual organization, or, more properly, a modern network with a decentralized cell structure. And so it remains. It has no fixed abode, with active members detectable in virtually every part of the world (its operatives are present in at least 100 countries, according to the Pentagon). Its essential infrastructure is a hard drive, and its organizational pathways are "built around a computer file".[126] The virtual qualities of revolutionary Islam grew, technologically speaking, from the laboratories of the new cyberworld and institutionally from the 1970s expansion of *al-da'wa* ("summons") in which clerics and preachers circulated their sermons as a mode of political action (its originary point

125   Al-Azmeh, *Islams and Modernities*, p. 27.
126   Gilles Kepel, *Jihad*, p. 315.

being al-Banna and the Muslim Brotherhood). The distribution of underground recordings early on created a "supranational focus", evident in the "considerable attention given to … the plight of Muslims worldwide".[127] New media, including satellite TV stations, newspapers distributed free on the Internet, news distribution through listserves, chat rooms and text messaging, and the traffic in CDs and DVDs, established the means to circumvent state censorship across the Middle East (and elsewhere in Islamdom) and an architecture capable of sustaining a transnational Arab multitude.

It is above all this extraordinary media transformation within the Arab world that revolutionary Islam has deployed to such effect. ("The Arab world" in this case includes the twenty or so million Muslims in the European Union.) The Web and Internet have been the central instruments in the creation of a virtual *umma*. They have erased the frontiers between *dar-al-Islam* (the land of believers) and *dar-al-Kufr* (the land of impiety), and created a new, and malignant, universalism – backed by the religious force of a *shari'a* and *fatwa* system imposed through the Internet. In seven years, the number of websites offering some form of support to the new Terror has grown from 12 to over 4,000.[128] Yahoo alone provides a home for over 200 jihad chat groups. There are two on-line magazines associated with al-Qaida (*Sawt al-Jihad* and *Muaskar al-Battar*) which feature articles for the novice insurgent on kidnapping, terrorist targets, and money-laundering.

Revolutionary Islam, to the extent that it is possible to chart its contours, seems to contain three main levels of virtual community: the message boards (for example *al Qal'ah* [the Fortress] and *al-Sahat* [the Fields]), the informational hubs (for example, Global Islamic Media),

127 Charles Hirschkind, "Civic Virtue and Religious Reason", *Cultural Anthropology*, vol. 16, no. 1, 2001, p. 11.
128 The sites are of course often transitory but see: www.aasam.com, www.jihadunspun.net, www.alowsaorg, www.drasat.com, www.7hj.7hj.com, www.qassam.net. See also John Robb's site: www.globalguerillas.typepad.com.

and the "mother sites" of the vanguard operatives (for example, *al-Faruq* [He who distinguishes Truth from Falsehood] and *Markaz al-Dirasat wal-Buhuth al-Islamiyyah* [the Center for Islamic Study and Research]). The mother sites are compelled to move several times a day to avoid capture, but they maintain their position by stealing unguarded server space (including, recently, that of the Arkansas Department of Highways) and sending out e-mails each day to inform the community of new links to the current site address. In this way, virtual Islam operates in a zone largely beyond the frontiers of regulation and detection.

In the early 1990s, many commentators were confident (most often gloatingly) that the public sphere in the Arab world was waning, even dying, as a result of the Gulf War and total American dominance in the region, of the Middle East "peace process", and of a general concentration of state power. "The impotence of the Arab street" became a leitmotif. Yet only a decade later, a new "Arabist community" has arisen, facilitated by the explosion of new media.[129] Islamic Jihad and al-Qaida cannot take all the credit for this, but radical Islam has contributed, in its tactical use of the likes of al-Jazeera and the virtual world, to the creation of a profound sense of collective suffering. Iraq, in the world of the websites, has come to stand for *all* Arabs and Muslims, and for the belief that the American occupation is aimed at Islam as a whole.

The virtual life, then, provides vanguard Islam with instantaneous connection, permitting unprecedented degrees of coordination and decentralized flexibility. A vast imagined community has come into being that feeds on the horrors of the *pax Americana*. The circulation of its propaganda, its image-making, its capacity to move financial resources (by some estimates a war chest running into billions of dollars) and to launder money (the illicit diamond business and the drugs trade are often its progenitors) are the new vanguard's hallmarks. These virtual structures

---

129 Marc Lynch, "Beyond the Arab Street", *Politics and Society*, vol. 31, no. 1, 2003, pp. 55–91.

hold together a complex constellation of militant internationalists – first and second generation jihadists war-hardened in Afghanistan, Bosnia, Somalia, and Chechnya and drawn from the entire Muslim arc from Morocco to the Philippines – but still tied to a particular locality. Already the Web has helped constitute what Olivier Roy calls Islamist "franchising".[130] Abu Musab al-Zarqawi's multinational guerilla organization Unity and Jihad morphs into al-Qaida in Mesopotamia; the North African cell Fizazi transmutes into the Moroccan Islamic Combatant Group; the al-Qaida Organization in the Arabian Peninsula [QAP] (*tanzim al-qa'ida fi jazirat al-arab*) is constituted by constantly mutating cells (the Haramain Brigades, the al-Quds and Falluja Squadrons) each with different identities, strategies, and tactics. A never-ending array of new vanguards – who on earth *are* the Servants of Allah the Powerful and the Wise now sending letters to *Le Monde*? – all detonate their home-made bombs under the al-Qaida "brand name".[131]

We have unearthed no startling new information on these terror networks, and our failure to do so makes us suspect that the State Department apparatchiks are similarly at a loss. One thing is incontestable, however. Four years after September 11, the long inventory of terrorist attacks makes a nonsense of the Bush administration's claim that al-Qaida is on the run (3,500 sympathizers have been detained, it is said, and 75 percent of the leadership killed). We lay our emphasis on the new vanguard's virtual qualities not simply because we are impressed by its deployment of satellite telephones, laptops, and encrypted websites. That way Orientalism lies. What matters is the way in which such technologies afford a vital meeting ground for millions of disaffected Muslims, and for

130 Olivier Roy, "Al-Qaida brand name ready for franchise", *Le Monde Diplomatique*, September 2004, p. 1, and Jessica Stern, *Terror in the Name of God*, New York 2003, pp. 237ff.
131 A last example would be Sarhane Ben Abdelmajid Fakhet, the Moroccan immigrant responsible for the Madrid bombings. They were carried out, so he said, in the name of the al-Andalus Brigade – al-Andalus being the Arabic name for the portion of Spain that fell to Muslim armies in 711.

the universalist aspirations (the global jihad) of the Islamic revolution-
aries themselves.

Here as elsewhere, dominance in the realm of the spectacle – which
is what we have just been describing – goes along with guns and high
explosive. In our discussion of Blood for Oil, we made much of the
privatization of the world armaments industry. We sought to link its
labyrinthine connectivity to the oil sector and to military neo-liberalism.
In relation to revolutionary Islam, the existence of a global arms market
leads in a different direction. A flourishing secondary market in
Kalashnikovs and AK-47s is the hallmark of the post-colonial failed
state. There is no match between the half-hearted attempts of authoritarian leaders to disarm civilian groups and the conspicuous ease with
which militants can now acquire weapons and ammunition. And what is
true for the automatic rifle is no less the case for the RPG or Stinger
missiles. Not to speak of nerve gas, anthrax, fissile material, and the like.

In the story of markets, states, and popular arsenals, a number of
forces are at work: the collusion between decrepit militaries and the
illegal weapons trade, the proliferation of private arms buyers flush with
oil money, the dumping of obsolete commodities in an industry marked
by constant innovation and a rising rate of destructive power. Add to this
the multiplication of Internet sites devoted to the construction and
employment of high-tech weaponry, and the ever-increasing *miniaturiza-
tion, portability,* and *invisibility* of explosive and bio-terror materials.[132]
The state, though it still commands airborne destruction, has lost its
monopoly on the means of violence. Let us recall that the operational
costs for the Jakarta bombing are estimated to have been $2,000, for
Madrid $1,000, for New York/Washington DC perhaps $175,000.

Perhaps too much has been made of cyber-terror in the current

---

132 The *Mujahadeen Poisons Handbook* (1996) by Abdel-Aziz is, for example, available on the
Hamas website. The much larger *Encyclopedia of Jihad* has been in circulation on the Net for
some time.

Photo: Jehad Nga/Corbis

Desktop background "wallpaper" (Amman, Jordan), child casualty, siege of Basra, 2003

proliferating literature on future netwars – the US troops in Afghanistan found engineering software, virtual models of dams, and computerized information on nuclear power plants, but no evidence of actual cyber-attacks in the planning stage – but the possibilities are real, nonetheless, and the attributes unequivocal: such warfare is cheap, anonymous, varied, remote, and potentially catastrophic. All of this, to sum up, has democratized the means of destruction. Radical Islam has been one of the process's prime beneficiaries.

Then, finally, to return to our starting point in approaching the present conjuncture, there is al-Qaida's mastery of (and obsession with) the world of appearances on TV. No one should imagine that the tactics of September 11 were other than long prepared, and carefully calibrated. The more we know of al-Qaida's history, the clearer its love affair with image-politics becomes.[133] The grave danger, noted al-Zawahiri, is of "volunteers getting killed in silence". Bin Laden returned to Saudi Arabia in the mid-1980s from Afghanistan as a popular hero. His war record continued to matter; but it was his adept use of Saudi media that eventually went to refute Prince Bandar's assessment of Osama at the time – that bin Laden could not "lead eight ducks across the street" – and marked his maturation as a propagandist.[134] Some of the most ferocious internal struggles within "the Base" have turned on the extent to which Egyptian cells resent Osama's TV persona – driven by the fact that al-Arabiya and al-Jazeera have become his mouthpieces. By now the symbiosis of revolutionary Islam and the perpetual emotion machines is unmistakable. *Fatwas* are routinely issued as grainy video-recordings; CDs circulate widely, and websites parade the vanguard leadership exhorting the faithful; the grisly beheadings are webcast. Al-Zawahiri and Osama bin Laden's post-September 11 video debriefing has Osama chuckling over his engineering expertise (his degree was awarded in public administration), extolling the martyrs, and reflecting on eighty years of Muslim humiliation. Its rhetorical and spectacular power was lost on no one. Just days after the attack, al-Qaida produced a promotional video – "The Big Job" – including a clever montage of lower Manhattan film footage set to victory music. QAP's highly professional media bureau employs a sophisticated virtual system to protect it from government surveillance and closure (which have plagued other websites). Since September 2003 it has published the bimonthly *Sawt al-Jihad* [the Voice of Jihad], a

---

133 On the al-Qaida laptop discovered in Afghanistan was a long history of visits by the Base operatives to a French website run by *Société Anonyme*, self-described as a "fluctuating group of artists and theoreticians who work specifically on the relations between critical thinking and artistic practices". The group also distributes the *Sabotage Handbook*.

134 Jonathan Randall, *Osama: The Making of a Terrorist*, New York 2004, pp. 90–2.

second bimonthly devoted to military affairs, and two high-quality martyr films depicting the process of preparing and executing the November 2003 attacks on the Muhayya compound in Saudi Arabia. We are witnessing the birth of a generation of militant *auteurs*. What better way to radicalize than through a vast image-world of sacrifice.

What we are pointing to in this new moment, then, is neither revolutionary violence in itself nor the fanaticism of its agents – the martyrs, the suicide bombers, the slaughtered children, the looted museums, the ravaged mosques – but the power deriving from the instantaneous circulation and consumption of images of these realities across the Islamic world. *Insofar as Hardt and Negri's "multitude" has constituted itself, thus far, as an enduring political force, its most visible face is that of the Islamic resistance.* Muslims around the globe have come to believe that the War on Terror is a war on their religion and way of life. So that even those clerics who condemned September 11 can now, four years later, fully support fighting against the occupation of Iraq. Given the disposition of virtual power over the last four years, Hosni Mubarak's prediction that the Iraq war would "create a hundred bin Ladens" comes to seem absurdly modest.

III

We wish to reiterate that revolutionary Islam is only one moment in the totality of Islamic politics. As with other political movements of a utopian cast – twentieth-century guerilla Marxism, for example, or sixteenth-century Protestant radicalism – a variety of tactics and strategies is employed by Islamists, from armed insurrection to building a parallel civil society, or to political parties operating within a parliamentary framework. Algeria – to take one case – has its fully militarized guerilla movements (remnant followers of the so-called *takfir al-mujtama* doctrine, which justified the horrors of the indiscriminate killing of civilians by the GIA in the 1990s), a raft of radical Islamist groups that have largely abandoned their utopian outlook and come to terms with the nation-state, three legal Islamist parties (the Movement of Society for Peace, the Movement of National Reform, and the Nahda Movement), and a large array of Islamic organizations – charities, service programs, schools, credit agencies – committed to the Islamization of society.

Islamism is multiform, then, and operates at many levels – the global *umma*, the territorially defined nation-state, the urban neighborhood, the kin group, or the tribe. This in part explains its appeal, its reach, and its astonishing political dynamism. One measure of those qualities is Islamism's huge library – mostly available on-line, naturally – dealing in detail with every topic under the sun: social justice, democracy, gender, human rights, government, banking, pedagogy (the interested reader may wish to consult www.muslim.org or www.islamtoday.net). And every effort by secular state managers to suppress or control such activity – in the name of freedom, needless to say, or the separation of church and state – unleashes a firestorm of Muslim protest. It is clear that within Muslim majority states at present, Islamists are the best organized and most effective political presence. They are adept at "organizing demonstrations, mobilizing civil society against structural adjustment, building and staffing schools, medical clinics and employment centers ... demanding charity for the poor, denouncing repression and torture ... constructing parallel institutions to dispense material, emotional and social support to those marginalized by the relentless march of global neo-liberalism".[135] In sum, they are the force that keeps Islamic society in being.

Over the last two decades, these movements have drawn strength from one fundamental fact: the presence of an actually existing Islamic

---

135 Paul Lubeck and Bryana Britts, "Muslim Civil Society in Urban Public Spaces", in J. Eade and C. Mele (eds), *Understanding the City*, Oxford 2002, p. 338, and Paul Lubeck, "Antinomies of Islamic Movements under Globalization", Center for Global, International and Regional Studies, University of California, Santa Cruz, *CGIRS Working Paper*, 1999, #99-1.

alternative to secular national development – that is to say, Muslim theocracy in Iran. It would be hard to exaggerate the significance of the 1979 Iranian Revolution. Here was an authentic Islamic uprising, the destruction of a massively militarized American client state, and the beginning of a grand political experiment in rule by jurists. Iran was a model for Muslims that resonated across sectarian and political lines. For contemporary Islamism, it was a founding moment. Here, said Sami Zubaida, was "an Islamic Revolution which was populist and anti-imperialist, which had spotted some of the vocabularies and slogans of the left, [but], unlike the 'imported' ideologies of Marxism or nationalism … was more accessible to the people, springing as it did from their historical cultural roots".[136]

No matter that the revolution obliterated the anti-imperialist Left, resorted immediately to the principle of revolutionary necessity, and deployed the absolute powers of the Islamic state with brutal effect – often in open contradiction to Islamic law. It was an exemplar, a blueprint, a home-grown alternative. Khomeini's regime was not a simple adoption of Qutbist radicalism: it represented a different revolutionary road altogether, extending the already formidable power of the lawgiver within Shi'ite theology. But it promoted, as did Qutb, the idea that sovereignty turns on Allah's exclusive right of legislation, that all law is divine, that Islamic governance resembles that of the Platonic philosopher-king, and that all secular authority is corrupt and idolatrous. Where Khomeini departed radically from the Qutbist model was in placing the Islamic rule of law under the guardianship of jurists (*fuqaha*). Many of the resulting innovations have diffused across the Shi'ite and Sunni mainstreams alike.

---

136 Sami Zubaida, *Islam, the People and the State*, London 1989, p. 56.

IV

What, then, finally, is the key to Islamism's success since the 1970s? Ideological energy and diversity are certainly part of it; so is the use made of the apparatus of spectacle; but on their own these realities explain too little. Two questions present themselves: Why the powerful wave of utopian Muslim militancy? And who are the recruits? Liberal analysis typically answers these questions in terms of the impact of modernization upon a tradition-bound *umma*. The Left occasionally reaches for its tattered copies of Fanon – explaining the paroxysm as an after-effect of empire, a revolt of still half-colonial subjects acting out of deep and abiding desperation. Our argument hinges rather on the *crisis of secular nationalist development* – abetted by a specific (and poisonous) political-economic conjuncture whose vectors were oil, primitive accumulation, and Cold War geopolitics.

We must begin in the sprawling mega-cities of the South – an urban archipelago of destitution and disenfranchisement. More than half the world's population now lives in cities, and 95 percent of the projected demographic growth over the next generation will be located in much the same fabric, spreading at the edges and clotting at its key centers. In the developing world, almost 50 percent of city-dwellers are housed in slums: in south-central Asia the figure is 58 percent, in sub-Saharan Africa it exceeds 70 percent.[137] The misery of life in Mumbai, Jakarta, or Lagos – each a holding-pen for populations in excess of ten million – is unprecedented. Within twenty-five years, the slum world is estimated to exceed two billion inhabitants.[138] Already in the ten most populous Muslim states, half the population is urban. By 2015 that will be true of more than two-thirds. And the city population is overwhelmingly young

---

137 *State of the World's Cities 2004/2005*, World Urban Forum, UN-Habitat, Barcelona 13–17 September 2004; *The Challenge of the Slums*, UN-Habitat, London 2003.
138 Mike Davis, "Planet of Slums", *New Left Review*, no. 26, 2004, pp. 5–34.

– the majority under thirty. (In Saudi Arabia, 45 percent are aged fourteen or under.)

This is the stage for the new politics of the Qu'ran Belt – in particular, for the crisis in the mega-cities of West Asia and Africa.[139] In contemporary Cairo, Amman, Kano, and Kuala Lumpur, a new public sphere is emerging in and around the Islamists' response to this developing urban reality – debating questions of legitimate rule, modernity, gender equality, social justice, and human rights. And political Islam's centrality to the process is all the more striking because it is essentially *uncontested* – because the secular state in the Muslim world has so signally abdicated its role as guide and arbiter of civil society.

The history of secular nationalism within West Asia and the realm of Islam turns on the fact that the modern nation-building project was in key respects stillborn. The experience of Ataturk's Turkey, Nasser's Egypt, and Pahlavi's Iran in the end dramatically disproved the notion that nationalism had put down real roots within Muslim society. Almost always the state apparatus and ideology had been imposed from above by bureaucratic nationalists and praetorian guards, and the nationhood that resulted had the look of a third-rate mimesis of the West. If certain Muslim monarchies (Saudi Arabia, Jordan, and the Gulf States) more readily accommodated Islam within the new state system, the legitimacy and solidity of their models of secular nationalism remained questionable. This whole brittle political infrastructure could not withstand the storm that struck in the wake of World War Two, and in particular the irresistible ascendancy of oil. The 1967 Arab–Israeli war and the crisis of import-substitution began the rot; but it was petro-capitalism,

---

139 Islamism, or revolutionary Islam, is in no simple sense the political voice of the ungoverned slum world. Selma Belaala may be quite right when he says that the suicide bombers and takfirists in Morocco are drawn from the *al-karyan* – the social outcasts scratching a living in the disused quarries of Meknes and Fez – but as, he also notes, several "theoreticians" implicated in the attacks were unquestionably the products of the professional classes. Selma Belaala, "Morocco: Slums Breed Jihad", *Le Monde Diplomatique*, November issue, 2004, p. 4–5.

neo-liberal austerity, and recession that finished the job. The very idea of modern secular development died with it. Modernity was – to return to Qutb – a condition of decay, a disenchanted world in need of redemption.

How exactly the oil boom of the 1970s played into the crisis of Arab nationalism is a complex story. Petro-capitalism proved to be a highly flammable mixture. The quadrupling of oil prices converted a number of Muslim states into fully fledged "oil nations". And oil-dependent economies, in spite of their vast wealth, soon proved to be among the most sordid, chaotic, and unjust of all polities. Oil states distinguish themselves each year by being ranked lowest in Transparency International's yearly inventory, the World Corruption Index. As the proportion of GDP accounted for by oil increases, economic underdevelopment, state corruption, and political violence grow in strict proportion. The so-called "paradox of plenty" is one of the few issues on which the IMF, Jeffrey Sachs, the human rights industry, the Catholic Church, and the millions of urban poor are in total agreement. How else can one interpret the squalid history of Nigeria: 400 billion oil dollars over forty years (1965–2004), $50 billion of which simply disappeared – leaving average standards of living at the start of the new century lower than at the moment of independence in 1960.

Saudi Arabia stands as the mother of Islamic petro-states. Its history is worth revisiting. The ruling monarchy had been petty chiefs of a poor, remote patch of desert until the 1740s, when they teamed up with a reformist preacher, Abd al-Wahhab (the father of Wahhabism). The fusion of Saud military might and *muwahhidun* fervor produced the unification of the Arabian Peninsula, but at a cost. In 1902 the Saud family, led by Abd al-Aziz Saud, wrestled control of Riyadh from his rivals, and, with the help of the British, won control of the region. Oil profits (for the companies as much as the House of Saud) required Islam. Any challenges to the regime – by labor in the 1950s, by frustrated Shi'ites in the

1970s, or by radical *sahwa* clerics in the 1990s – were met with a monarchical iron fist (and latterly by American troops).

The first oil boom shunted trillions of dollars directly into state coffers (the Saudis pocketed over $300 billion between 1973 and 1980). Fiscal centralization and state-led economic expansion produced not turbo-charged laissez-faire but a rank crony capitalism. Political classes distributed contracts to clients and patrons, promoting quixotic industrial ventures, all in the name of modernization. The construction boom sucked millions of people from the countryside just as inflation, land speculation, and endemic corruption crippled what remained of the urban moral economy. Oil shocks turned the ossified Muslim monarchies and city-states into theatres of petro-decadence; even a minor prince, said one Saudi architect, is entitled to a $40 billion palace. Building this country, said Prince Bandar, "we corrupted $50 billion [sic] ... So what? We didn't invent corruption".

At the same time, the wider territory of Islam was feeling the effects of the oil boom.[140] The 1970s had shifted vast dollar resources to the Saudi and Gulf States, sucking in more than 20 million workers to labor on sumptuary projects – golf courses and irrigated wheat fields in the desert – thereby exposing a large multicultural migrant Muslim labor force to Islamist doctrines. Pakistani, Indian, Philippino, Afghan, Egyptian, and Tunisian workers were tossed together in a rainbow labor market that served as a perfect incubator for Islamic radicalism. The region's petro-dollars funded global networks of Islamic associations, charities, banks, mosques, and, as we now know, vanguardist cells across the Muslim world. Bin Laden senior, a Yemeni expatriate contractor and acolyte of King Saud, turns out to have been a paradigmatic case of oil wealth at work.

---

140 Buoyant oil prices during 2004 will bring yet another bonanza to the Gulf States; OPEC's annual revenues for the year are estimated to be in the order of $360 billion.

The crash of petroleum prices in the mid-1980s (from almost 41 to 8 dollars a barrel between 1981 and 1985) put an end to what remained of secular nationalism. Collapsing state revenues, expanded public borrowing, and painful debt servicing all began to spiral out of control, as each encountered the first punishments of "structural adjustment". The cities of Islamdom, now crammed with rural migrants, international workers, and unemployable university graduates, descended into penury. The World Bank and Wall Street finished what the boom had begun. Devaluation, privatization, the elimination of state subsidies, the withdrawal of basic needs programs – this was suddenly the music of the new urban world.

Secular nation-states within the shatterbelt of oil enjoyed a number of obvious common features – dictatorship, religious oppression, corruption, and failed development. Ataturk, Boumedienne, Nasser, Sukarno, Asad, Hussein: the names came to stand for what seemed a necessary association between secularism and repression, between the idea of Progress and the "nationalization" of Islam. As the secular state withered under neo-liberal pressure – and on occasion, as in Somalia, collapsed outright – Muslim civil society filled the vacuum of state failure.

And there is one last (fatal) element to the story – namely, the Cold War. The long-term impact of that reality on the Middle East has figured largely throughout the book. But from the point of view of Islamic activism, the Cold War can be said to have come to a head at the end of the 1970s. Its defining events were the Camp David accord between Egypt and Israel, signed in 1979; the Iranian Revolution; and the Soviet invasion of Afghanistan. In them and through them, the US emerged as the jihadists' real enemy – the process assisted, as everyone now knows, by America's arming and support of the war against godlessness in Afghanistan. Somalia, Bosnia, Chechnya, and the Taliban's training camps acted as a transnational forcing house for what al-Zawahiri called "a new phenomenon": young combatants who "abandon their families, countries, property, studies and jobs to seek a place in which to carry out jihad".[141] Add to this the presence of US military bases close to the Holy of Holies, the continuing nightmare in Gaza and the West Bank, and Bush Senior's betrayal of the Shi'ite uprising against Saddam in 1991. The stench of American complicity in the rise of Islamism is overpowering.

V

We have now sketched our view of modern Islamism and its relation to the crisis of secular national development. It is a picture, we reiterate, of a distinctively modern political movement – with the revolutionary vanguard only one of its many facets. But finally, inevitably, it is to a judgment of the vanguard we must turn.

We are witnessing a real resistance to empire – and with it, once again, a yoking of history and cruelty that now has the opportunity to stage a daily spectacle of its doings. (And to resist the slightest spectacular deviation from its own line: as we write, news arrives of the bombing of al-Arabiya's headquarters in Baghdad by the 1920 Brigades, with an Internet posting denouncing the network's reporters as "Americanized spies speaking in Arabic".) We reject the new militants' cult of Terror, for reasons we go on to specify in the chapter that follows; and we have no reason to believe that the vanguard Islamists' selection (and interpretation) of texts will lead them finally to a politics adequate to the times. But it is not helpful, in our view, to label the vanguardists "fascist". Al-Qaida and its like have no foundation in organic nationalism, racial superiority, or even charismatic leadership. Their call to arms is universalist, multicultural, and internationalist – claiming to represent a global

---

141 Ayman al-Zawahiri, "Knights under the Prophet's Banner", in Laqueur, *Voices of Terror*, p. 427.

umma.[142] And nothing in the nature of political Islamism in general dictates, as we see it, a vanguard and Terrorist solution to the problem of history. Alongside al-Qaida, political Islamism in its hour of triumph has produced – and is still producing – all manner of gradualist, non-violent forms of democratic inclusion. In the wake of the defeat of the jihadist factions in Egypt, for example, a number of former Brothers established a new centrist political party, *Hizb al-Wasat*, in 1996. It grew from radical reconfigurations within the Muslim Brotherhood itself, and specifically renounced the resort to jihad – recognizing Egypt, at last, as a Muslim country with an (imperfect) Islamic polity. Even in Saudi Arabia, the state has opened a national dialogue in which a number of militants and *sawha* preachers have recanted or condemned acts of violence, and established a space – still fragile and circumscribed – in which a loose coalition of progressive Sunni and Shi'ites can operate. There is (as the worried think-tanks go on reassuring us) an emerging opposition to the vanguard within the wider Islamic world. The on-line sermons of Shaykh Yusuf al-Qaradwi, the new voices within the Iranian Shi'ite establishment, the brave arguments of the Indonesian scholar Harun Nasution, the Moroccan philosopher Muhammed Abdel al-Jabri, and the Egyptian cleric Gama al-Banna – these are signs pointing the way. Whether they will be followed remains to be seen.

As for the revolutionary Islamists, they can be said to have beaten Bush at his own game: faith-based service provision and regime change (in Madrid). Their pragmatism and discipline remain chilling. And the conditions that created them – the ruin of the secular nation-state, the liquidation of Left politics in the Muslim world (or of critical secularism

---

142 Islam, in a word, has its own version of "globalization", which builds on the centuries-old cosmopolitanism of pilgrimage, mission, and *caravanserai. Jihad*, in turn, is no respecter of nation-state boundaries. And this new international perspective has been sharpened by the fact, or perception, that Islam now faces an enemy with a global perspective of its own. To call this a clash of civilizations is overdramatic. Neo-liberalism is not a "civilization": it is a set of interests rightly perceived as inimical to those of the Muslim world.

of almost any kind), the ongoing disaster of "urbanization"[143] – intensify, if anything, as the years pass.

Qutb's two guiding ideas remain basic. Modernity has revealed itself as a state of deep social and moral decay, and Islam itself is in immediate danger. It is hard to imagine any circumstances in which these ideas could have been more dramatically confirmed than those of the past two years in Iraq. Military occupation, the bombing and strafing of tens of thousands of civilians, the attacks on the Najaf Cemetery and other holy sites, the degradations of Abu Ghraib – all the horrors of the current phase of America's permanent war – have corroborated, under the constant supervision of the spectacle, the truth of the vanguard's assessment of the unbelievers.

---

143 Muhammad Atta waxed lyrical in his Hamburg University thesis on the Aleppo *souk*, under siege, in his view, from tourists, fast-food restaurants and ugly hotels. It was the American skyscraper that symbolised for him the shameless greed of those who sought to violate the integrity of the old Aleppo.

Demonstration, London, 2004

6

MODERNITY AND TERROR

The instinct that drives them away from modern reality is unassailable – what do we care that they have chosen a retrograde short cut! The essential thing about them is not that they want to go "back": but rather, that they want to get – away. A bit more strength, lightness, courage, artistry: and they would want to get up and out – and not go back!

—Nietzsche, *Beyond Good and Evil*

We do not begin this final chapter with Nietzsche because we agree with him, but because he addresses the current predicament – the eternal predicament, of modernity and those who oppose it – full in the face, even if his Nietzschean gaiety by way of response is ultimately fatuous. Things are far worse than Nietzsche could ever have imagined. His vision of Last Man happiness, which haunted our Introduction – a future in which "everybody wants the same, everybody is the same, and whoever feels different goes voluntarily into an asylum" – seems to miss the full horror of the present turn. Last Man happiness is still under construction, and the inch-deep unanimity it promises is still the ultimate (and proximate) dystopia. But who would have dreamt, even as recently as five years ago, that the Prozac state would so rapidly reveal itself as the Empire of Shock and Awe? Who could have seen in advance that the blinking contentment of the twenty-first-century image-world would be more and more shadowed by a worldwide, merciless Will to Go Back? And a Will that has proved itself able, centrally, to take advantage of the very Last Man technology – the apparatus of spectacle – that it is dedicated to destroying.

We intend this conclusion to be Nietzschean only in the following sense: that it aim to understand the paroxysm of September 11 and after as yet another in the endless sequence of crises of modernity itself; that it not be baffled or panicked by the return of the old, the backward, and the atavistic, come to interrupt the consumers' feast; and that it see the recrudescence of the past as speaking to the truth of the modernity we have – the fake presentness, the even more fraudulent dream of a time to come – and therefore push relentlessly at what it is, in recurrent "humanity", that is being mobilized again. The title of the great third treatise of Nietzsche's *On the Genealogy of Morals*, in which he pulls together the threads of his analysis of religion, is "What Do Ascetic Ideals Mean?" We believe that the Left in present circumstances, faced with the phenomenon of al-Qaida, can contribute to future politics only if it poses Nietzsche's question again; and in a form that touches uncomfortably on the Left's own past. "What Does The Vanguard Ideal Mean?": that is the question. (Or, "What Does It Mean To Be Militant?" Or, "Why Does Leninism Never Die?") Why is it that human beings, faced with the cruelty and disappointment of the present, seem drawn ineluctably to one or another version of the warrior ideal (or the warrior crossed with the flagellant): to a dedication to hardness, ruthlessness, fierce bonding, closure against the mereness of the everyday; to a dedication finally to Death – to the making, the forcing, of history, and the rewriting of the future according to the script of some dismal Messiah?

We realize the dangers here. The last thing we intend to do in what follows is reduce the Islamic world's resistance to modernity to the one model of Unity and Jihad. Islamism in its present forms, still mutating and metastasizing in the slum conurbations of the World Bank world, is very far from being a vanguard movement alone. We shall return to this. For the moment, let us simply say – as we have repeatedly throughout the book – that the phenomenon of al-Qaida is unavoidable, fundamental. Islamism is not to be equated with its revolutionary vanguard; but never, alas, has the world presented such a classic breeding ground for the vanguard ideal as the billion new city-dwellers of Asia and North Africa. Classic, but also unprecedented. Never before have the human materials which the vanguard aims to mobilize (and sacrifice) existed on such a scale, and in such a state of unregenerate misery and disorientation. And never before – this is the truly chilling reality – have the wretched of the earth existed in such a bewildering and enraging hybrid state, with the imagery of consumer contentment piped direct into slum dormitories rented out by the night, at cutthroat prices, to hopelessly indebted neo-serfs.

Readers will recall that Nietzsche is very far from dismissing the great fact he is trying to confront: he wishes to understand the purpose – not just the appeal, but the historical function – of the urge to life-denial and self-abnegation that has so dominated humans' thinking about themselves. The Left should approach al-Qaida in the same spirit – with the words and actions of bin Laden resonating against those of Lenin, Blanqui, Mao, Baader-Meinhof, and Durruti. The vanguard ideal had a function, obviously: its narrowness and secretiveness and merciless instrumentalism in the face of human subjects answered, however distortedly, to a set of actual conditions – possibilities – for reassembling our (always) afflicted Powers. *The vanguard ideal was an understandable response to the reality imaged on our frontispiece* – the reality of history. That it was understandable does not mean that it was any the less disastrous, for the victim on the box as much as for those who were working, at the same moment, to build a politics in which the "victim" might become the agent of change – as opposed to one more anonymous bondman, in the great procession of the hooded, always about to be led by Moses into the promised land. We dream of an answer to "What Does The Vanguard Ideal Mean?" which would hold in balance a loathing for the ideal – and a sense that in al-Qaida it has found its perfect and (we hope) terminal expression – and a comprehension of the forces that gave rise to it.

I

We dream of an answer. Of course we are aware that the problems pointed to thus far in the present chapter are deeply intractable, and not likely to be properly articulated, let alone solved, in the space of twenty pages. They are the questions that have come up, somewhat against our will, in the course of exploring the more specific and "conjunctural" issues that rightly dominate most of the book. They offer the kind of perspective, we are convinced, within which the problems of the new age of Terror will have to be viewed in a politics to come – especially if there is to be the least hope of a Left alternative to the War in Heaven. We shall pose the questions, in other words, not answer them. Or rather, we shall offer answers in a speculative, aphoristic vein – answers as *beginnings*, of an argument on the Left which we think it urgent to provoke.

Let us start again from the circumstances of the past four years. What are the moment's defining features? On the one side, a resurgent imperialism, with "modernity" and "democracy" its watchwords, replacing the old promise of "civilization". And a sovereign power at the center of things that no longer hesitates to declare unending War its *raison d'être*, and to push toward a ghost form of government – a second and authoritative polity – in which secrecy is of the essence and bureaucracy is not required to answer, even formulaically, to the rule of law. The *first* polity of this sovereign power – and no one is denying the continuing necessity to the US of control in the non-secret realm – is more and more attuned to the cluster of techniques and priorities called spectacle; and therefore less and less able to tolerate the possibility of spectacular defeat. But that is the condition it has lived, at least partly, since September 11; and its response to the new circumstances – in the Middle East, above all – has driven it closer to a situation in which spectacular defeat may be compounded by (in a sense, may precipitate) real strategic failure. It remains unclear – putting the matter as dryly as we dare – how the brutalities of primitive accumulation can be properly attended to in the age of al-Jazeera and the torturer with the Toshiba PDR.

To boast in front of Parliament, as Churchill did in 1920, that "I do not understand this squeamishness about the use of gas .... I am strongly in favour of using poisoned gas against uncivilized tribes [to] spread a lively terror": this is one thing.[144] Honorable members will understand you, even if they disagree. (Liberal imperialism never dies.) The situation is somewhat different, it seems to us, if the platitudes of liberation are trotted out – even to an audience of Labour/Republican sycophants – when every night on TV a naked man is crying on the end of a leash.

And in response? Surely nothing the world should be *surprised* at. The latest mutation of the vanguard ideal – often drawing its personnel and basic organizational ideas direct from the failed Leninisms of a few years before. A globalized guerilla, in love with new media, drunk on secrecy, believing in a world of "bases" with an equal and opposite fervor to that of its opponent.

We have rarely been closer to hell on earth. That we have thought it worthwhile to write about politics at all, in such circumstances, derives from the fact – here is where *Afflicted Powers* started – that there is one potential positive in the past years to weigh against the deadly

---

144 Quoted in Geoff Simons, *Iraq: From Sumer to Saddam*, New York 1994, p. xiv. Churchill was Secretary of State at the War Office in 1920, and was defending his authorization of RAF Middle East Command to use chemical weapons "against recalcitrant Arabs".

complementaries. Real agents of opposition to the present state of things have come into being, often taking on forms that no one remotely predicted: above all, the unlooked-for pattern of resistance to globalization, North and South, that has changed the landscape of neo-liberalism over the past decade; and which prepared the way for, and inevitably (in the North) was overtaken by, the great mobilization against the war. We return to these struggles in our final pages. Let us simply say here that this movement, or movement of movements, shows no sign of abating. It will be doomed to repeat itself, for obvious reasons. There will be many more wars to prevent, and enclosures to break down. Therefore we make no excuses for having stuck close, in the body of the book, to the images and arguments of the day – September 11, revolutionary Islam, Israel and Palestine, oil, and the warfare state. The multitude will inevitably go on grappling with these realities for years to come. We have wanted to offer some different ways of doing so.

But this on its own is not enough. Behind the immediate bad weather of politics lies a pattern of global warming – a change in the average temperature of modernity. If the Left is to survive as a political entity, as we have said before, it will have to speak meteorologically. Al-Qaida is not a passing storm. This is why we return to our Nietzschean question.

And multiply it by two. The question "What Does The Vanguard Ideal Mean?" cannot be properly answered, in present circumstances, without broaching a second: "How Are We To Understand The Present Form Of Modernity (and hence the present form of resistance to it)?"

We take the questions in reverse order. Even to tackle the question of modernity, we realize, is to risk the worst kind of imprecision and over-reach – to end up producing the usual (useless) theory of everything. We shall begin as we did in the case of spectacle, with minimal and matter-of-fact descriptions; making no effort to disguise these descriptions' partiality, and focusing on the aspects of the modern condition which we believe are key to revolutionary Islam's rejection of it. What we should like to move toward, ultimately – or at least intimate, at least set out the bare coordinates of – is an opposition to modernity having nothing in common with al-Qaida's, even while recognizing what it is in modernity that provokes the al-Qaida response. A non-orthodox, non-nostalgic, non-rejectionist, non-apocalyptic critique of the modern: that ought now to be the task of Left politics. Otherwise the ground of opposition to the present will be permanently ceded to one or another fundamentalism.

Exactly when in human history there emerged the first societies no longer oriented toward the past – toward the preservation of continuities, the worship of ancestors, the safe transmission of Word or Sign – is never likely to be agreed on. Why it happened, ditto. That it happened remains the great (and maddening) thing. Certain societies left the past behind, or tried to, and began to pursue a projected future – of goods, pleasures, freedoms, forms of control over nature, infinities of information. The process was accompanied by a terrible emptying and sanitizing of the imagination. For without the Word, without the imagined and vivid intricacies of kinship, without the past living on (most often monstrously) in the detail of everyday life, meaning became a scarce commodity – if by "meaning" we have in mind agreed-on and instituted forms of value and understanding; orders implicit in things; stories and images in which a culture is able to crystallize its sense of the struggle with the realm of necessity and the realities of pain and death. The phrase Max Weber borrowed from Schiller, "the disenchantment of the world" – gloomy yet in our view exultant, with its promise of a disabused dwelling in the world as it is – still sums up this side of modernity best.

Gloomy and exultant. The problem for Left politics lies precisely here: in the peculiar difficulty, so it turns out, of keeping these two necessary valences alive in the same description. Left accounts of modernity end up almost invariably on one side or another of the great divide: Jeremiads against the commodity and all its works, or pallid cheerleading for a technical utopia just itching to emerge (yet again) from the bonds of outdated "relations of production". Things are at their worst when the Left confronts "consumerism" or "consumer society". Even Jeremiah can seem sunny in comparison. We too lack enthusiasm for home-shopping channels and the Mall of America; but the point is to understand the powers and insufficiencies of a form of life – to understand why it carries the world before it, and why people are willing to die to prevent its doing so – not to wallow in its pathos.

We shall try. Let us accept that consumerism – the gearing of commodity production (of course not exclusively, but in ways that genuinely alter the tempo and structure of economic life) to the provision of disposable, "personal", fashion-stamped goods – is the form of capitalism now presenting itself, worldwide, as the threshold to the future. And that as a vision of desirable life it has at present no rival; or no rival that does not promise a Going Back, a sloughing off of appetite and futurity altogether. It is a *vision* – let us accept that, however reluctantly. That is, it offers its adepts a seeming solution to the disenchantment of the world: it promises to fill the life-world with meanings again, with magical answers to deep wishes, with models of having and being and understanding (undergoing) Time itself. It is the false *depth* of consumerism that drives its opponents to distraction, and into the arms of the vanguard. They sense that in the form of "consumer society" capitalism has truly and fully become a way of life, as opposed to a (dazzling) set of means and relations of production. To call consumerism a religion, then (which is one of its enemies' standard moves), is to say something serious, though not quite accurate. Consumerism (as Marx famously glimpsed) is more like a new form of totemism – taking that last word entirely without condescension. It promises a world in which possessable and discardable objects do the work of desiring and comprehending for us, forming our wishes, giving shape to our fantasies, making matter signify.

There is no mystery to such a vision's appeal. It plays on a deep (maybe constitutive) human disposition to invest the manipulation of objects with magic power; it offers a solution to a fundamental meaning-deficit in the world as it is; and at present it lacks competition, if what we are looking for is alternative models of what to do with capitalism's productive potential – what to do *humanly*, that is; in the service of which version of the human our assembled capacities might be put to use. We have reached a strange moment, when it is necessary to state in the most basic terms what is wrong – what is radically insufficient – with the consumer society's promise.

Again, no Jeremiads. Personal objects, including mass-produced objects, will necessarily go on being one main instrumentation of meaning and desiring in any human society we care to imagine. But they cannot and do not work the magic they are presently called on to perform. Commodities can embody human purposes, and are capable of inflecting and developing such purposes, only if they are constantly subject to reorientation – change of function, change of valuation, *recall to their mere instrumentality* – in a world of meanings vastly exceeding those that any *things* can conjure up. Objects cannot be the preeminent form in which objectives are pictured and needs articulated. In particular, objects cannot do this kind of work if they are standardized, with "personal" signatures added as icing on the cake. And they cannot do such work if their magic depends increasingly, as it does in consumer society, on their (fantastical) separation from the human – their being-together in a world where they seem almost to make meanings on their own, answering not to their users but to others of their kind, with more and more of the commodity action happening in a supercharged, oneiric realm of appearance.

Of course the actual producers of this realm of appearance recognize, in practice, all the insufficiencies we have outlined. They are realists. They know full well that commodities can only borrow real human powers, human qualities, from the world they pretend to perfect and surpass. And so the spectacle – for what we have been describing is one (central) part of it, devoted to making commodities desirable – is endlessly parasitic on the values of a vanishing sociality. It injects its objects with homeopathic doses of "community", "respect for tradition", decency, loyalty, tenderness, naivety, eccentricity, caring – in a word, love. The operation is deadly. It travesties the values it cannibalizes. In order for "caring" and "loving" and "being with others" to be attached, as values, to minor variants in home furnishings or electronic data processors, the values in question have to be emptied of the least difficulty, the least recalcitrance. What is most depressing about consumerism, then, is not that it fails to deliver on its promise of happiness – that is what makes opposition possible – but that in the process it works endlessly to eviscerate the materials out of which human happiness (and recognition of unhappiness) might still be built.

Yes, yes – in the end we have failed to stifle our distaste. And we never intended to: the point was to move step by step to a level where real hostility might be possible, as opposed to lofty dismissal. Which brings us back to al-Qaida. Revolutionary Islam, we have been arguing, is a movement born in revulsion from many particular facets of the modern condition. It struggles with the legacies of colonialism, and with the current return of the colonial repressed; it thrives on the agonized failure of the secular state; it has a language – here is where the archaism of its anger may prove its greatest strength – for the horror of the neo-liberal townscape. But again what matters in al-Qaida's makeup is the mixture of atavism and new-fangledness. Its best recruits are refugees from exactly the world of goods (and gadgets) we have been describing. Among its various apprenticeships to modernity, then, revolutionary Islam *has been obliged to suffer the full force of consumerism* – to suffer it in a way (with an intensity) that is only possible for those living in societies where consumerism is still part reality, part dream of a future to come.

Avon Lady with deodorant sample, Brazil, 2002

The Islamists' rage and contempt for the modern "Life" they go on savaging in their communiqués will never be understandable until what they have suffered – what they have lived through – is taken seriously again.

This goes in particular for the model of *temporality* that consumerism offers its subjects (since it is above all a different model of past, present, and future that stands at the center of al-Qaida's rejection of the West).

We are close to the heart of the matter. Modernity, particularly in its consumer society manifestation, is less and less able to offer its subjects ways to live in the present, and to have the flow of time be accepted and inhabited as it happens. And this is precisely because it stakes everything on celebrating – perpetuating – the here and now. Lately it has built an extraordinary apparatus to enable individuals to image, archive, digitalize, objectify, and take ownership of the passing moment. The here and now is not endurable, it seems (or at least, not fully real), unless it is told or shown, immediately and continuously, to others – or to oneself. The cell-phone, the digital replay, instant messaging, "real time" connectivity, the video loop. Far be it from us – image-lovers to a fault – to say that giving an experience visual form means not living it. It depends on what the imaging is for. But there is a kind of visualization, we all know in our bones (and common parlance is often scathing on the subject), that is essentially a mechanism of defense – a way of deliberately alienating the moment, and putting the *non-lived*, the *non-significant*, at a distance. The spectacle, we have been arguing, is a social process that is hollow at the core. The reality it offers its subjects is that of Reality TV. And its subjects are always in flight from this emptiness, even as – especially as – they snort their line of nothingness with the true user's delight in all the latest paraphernalia. We shall return to this.

Consumer culture is many-faceted. For example, the gadgetry of instant objectification is nowadays accompanied by a wider realm of commodity appearance – in advertising, design, the whole staging of commodity life in commercials and info-tainment – more and more oriented to the past. Once upon a time what commodities promised was the future, above all. Now a whole (dominant) class of them exists to invent a *history*, a lost time of togetherness and stability, that everyone claims to remember but no one quite had. It is a short step from this omnipresent pseudo-memory to a "nostalgia for the present"[145] – the stylized display of the latest fashions and accessories as if they already possessed the glamor of the outdated. And so on. The wheel of false temporality spins faster and faster.

145 See Fredric Jameson, "Nostalgia for the Present", *South Atlantic Quarterly*, vol. 88, Spring 1989, pp. 517–37, and Arjun Appadurai, "Consumption, Duration, and History", in Appadurai, *Modernity at Large: Cultural Dimensions of Globalization*, Minneapolis and London 1996, pp. 66–85.

Our purpose is not to enter into the detail of consumer metaphysics – we lack courage for that – but, again, to understand what opposition to such metaphysics amounts to. We think it is rooted in a crisis of time. For what is the current all-invasive, portable, minute-by-minute apparatus of mediation we have pointed to if not an attempt to expel the banality of the present moment – the dim actuality of what is happening – from consciousness? It will be given a separate, *disownable* form on the spot. And therefore it will be forgotten. The whole point of the unlooked-at videos and never-downloaded digital photocards is their invisibility: they are the experience we all wish to pretend we never had; they are the non-present we aim to forget as we punch its coordinates into the palm pilot; always with the underlying hope that in doing so *another* present – a present with genuine continuities with a retrieved past, and therefore one opening onto some *non-empty, non-fantastical* vision of the future – will come to be in its place.

So … the endless enthusiasm of the modern for imaging devices – devices of displacement and distancing – needs further interpretation. Certainly it constitutes submission to a new technics of the spectacle; and we are not denying that the pervasiveness of this submission – its urgency, its ubiquitousness, its taken-for-grantedness – produces problems for power. The ordinary horror and shamefulness of *enforcement* will be recorded too easily and too often: it has to be recorded, since experience without instant doubling *is* no experience at all. "Here's me third from the left at Thanksgiving in Abu Dhabi; and here's me on top of a pigpile of Terrorists."

But the ultimate question, we have been arguing, is not so much the side-effects of the submission to the image-world as what the submission is in search of – what it desires, what it can never find. Somewhere here lies the answer to the question: What is it, most deeply, that modernity's enemies do not want? Those who say that what they recoil from is change, or freedom, or self-invention, or endless openness, have it exactly wrong. What revolutionary Islam cannot stomach – what it feels already arriving in the engorged cities it uses as hiding-place – is the idea of a human existence *without a present tense*.

II

What, then, does the vanguard ideal mean? Maybe now we can frame an answer. We take the question to be ultimately one of political psychology (an underdeveloped art): meaning that what has to be explained is the depth and intensity of the ideal's hold on individual subjects; and, above all, why the ideal makes more converts, not less, as modernity lives on.

We realize, naturally, that the vanguard ideal is in some sense a muta-tion of very ancient, maybe primordial forms of human bonding. But it is precisely wrong to see it as a barbarism or regression. The vanguard ideal is a modern phenomenon – even, *especially*, in its wish not to be. What does the vanguard ideal mean? Here is the militant's reply:

I have chosen *not to be modern*; and only I have a proper estimate of what it takes, minute by minute, to make that choice real. I have built a life-world which is truly the negation – the strict, obsessive, point-by-point inversion – of the modern life I once had.

I embrace the finite and bonded as opposed to the formless. I choose self-sacrifice as opposed to self-satisfaction, and hardness and cruelty as opposed to complaisance. I close myself against all but the narrowest range of messages, and those messages I repeat to myself endlessly, and deeply internalize – in flight from the lightness, the thinness and exteri-ority, of "belief" in modern conditions. Denial will be my God, not appetite. The planned and ritualized will put paid to contingency. Last Man happiness will mean nothing to me. Suicide (that most modern of negations) will be my *telos*, and I reserve my deepest scorn for the enemy's instituted non-recognition of death. I pursue the *unmediated* – the act, the killing, the pure flame of destruction – as antidote to what you moderns are living, and do not know how desperately you wish to escape from: the endless reel of representation. "Violence shall synchronize my movements like a tune,/ And Terror like a frost shall halt the flood of thinking."[146]

Several unwelcome conclusions follow. The vanguard of Terror is at present modernity's only adequate opposition – a vicious and fantastical one, no doubt, but in these very qualities speaking to the truth of modernity in ways no language of Reason dares to. And the vanguard has the future in its bones. The purer and more asphyxiating the condition of modernity becomes, the more powerful the vanguard's appeal – not essentially as a political tactic, but *as a form of life*.

This is no doubt gloomy reading, but it is not a message of despair. It means to point the Left to what vanguardism is, why it is renascent, and on what level – in the longer term – battle with it will have to be joined. At the level of modernity, is the proposal. In the setting out (to repeat our previous characterization) of a non-nostalgic, non-anathematizing, non-regressive, non-fundamental, non-apocalyptic critique of the modern. The Left has a long way to go even to lay the groundwork of such a project – and the recent small flood of enthusiasm for the "virtual" has pointed it in exactly the wrong direction – but it is still only from the Left that a real opposition to modernity could come.

These are, we insist, actual and pressing questions raised by the present crisis – not matters to be left to one side till Bush/Blair is defeated and the boys come home. Even Wolfowitz and Geoff Hoon are now saying that the War on Terror will ultimately be fought and won in the realm of "ideology". Of course what they believe to be the West's best weapon in

146 W. H. Auden, "In Time of War", *The Collected Poetry of W. H. Auden*, New York 1945, p. 342.

this struggle is precisely the reality – the dream of consumer spectacle – we have been describing. They may even be right. Of course it is likely that many more people in Mosul or Jakarta will want washing machines and laptops than will opt for the future Unity and Jihad has to offer. The vanguard ideal is the realm of the few. It is a rearguard action. But the point is that it will prove a *permanent* rearguard action, feeding on the energies of the new city proletariat, and one that will go on *determining the paranoid form of modernity adopted in response to it*, unless modernity itself is called in question.

III

We return to the surface features of the past few years, and now try to sum them up. Many pages ago we proposed the terms "atavism and new-fangledness" to point to the present temper of politics, and they have come up again *apropos* al-Qaida. Atavism, the reader will now realize, is tied in our view to a central new set of capitalist imperatives – a pattern of needs and failures and necessities, which we have tried to outline, as a result of which a fresh round of primitive accumulation is being attempted. The turn is necessary – "There's soon going to be nowhere in the mineral extraction heartland where we can do business" is the judgment underlying it – but obviously it carries a high degree of risk. Primitive accumulation (in the world as it is) means *war*; and war is the maker of empires, but also the breaker. Primitive accumulation means war; but one fought now in unprecedented conditions – an armed struggle partly impelled by, and continuing to be fought in, that complex of circumstances we call spectacle. For new-fangledness, then, substitute the war of websites, the ballistic exchange of images, the battle to maintain (or put an end to) weak citizenship.

No doubt it is true that the present fiasco in Iraq bears witness to incompetence and lack of forethought on many levels. The planners were so dazzled by the Revolution in Military Affairs that it never dawned on them that no Revolution in Occupation Affairs had accompanied it (for all Israel's thirty-five-year attempt to create one). They fed on the lies of their expatriate assets. They chose to ignore what their own policy of sanctions had done to the "secular", sophisticated, West-leaning civil society they went on dreaming was waiting in the wings. And so on. The litany is familiar. But no lack of preparedness was more profound than the military's in confronting the new world of instant – and disputed – mediation. Brigadier General Mark Kimmitt, at that time the senior military spokesman in Iraq, was asked on April 11, 2004 – as the first major offensive against the occupation was unfolding – what he would tell Iraqis in the face of televised images "of Americans and coalition soldiers killing innocent civilians". "Change the channel", was his reply. "Change the channel to a legitimate, authoritative, honest news station."[147]

Primitive accumulation is to be carried out in conditions of spectacle: that is the new reality in a nutshell. And the spectacle itself, we have been arguing, is in the process of mutation. A new round of technical innovation has made alienation-into-a-realm-of-images a pervasive, banal, *constantly self-administered* reality. The dystopian potential of such an apparatus is sufficiently clear. But in present circumstances it has at least the benign side-effect of making control of the spectacle by the state – the kind of short-term and absolute control of imagery that is a necessity of war and occupation, as opposed to the tendential and structural "management" of appearances appropriate to peacetime – truly hard to maintain.

This destabilization of the spectacle has been accompanied by an even more bizarre turn of events with regard to the spectacle as a territory of *belief* – as something its users and occupiers psychically invest in, and whose imagery of the future they assent to. Twenty years ago, one of us

---

147   *New York Times*, April 12, 2004.

remembers being told by a shrewd observer that the new cyber-technology then becoming available would change the whole confidence and aggressivity of the white-collar class. "You wait and see. The bourgeoisie is about to fall in love with the future again." So it proved; and for two decades the dream of the digital went largely unchallenged. Who could have predicted, even five years ago, the swiftness and completeness with which the dreaming became a thing of the past? Now no one under thirty entertains the least illusion about what their drab courses in computer science will lead to. They are a ticket to data-punching, if you are lucky – if the job you have been trained for is not outsourced to Bangalore before you graduate. No wonder the actual *subjects* of the information world regard the hustlers and hucksters of cyberspace – the fifty-year-olds who go on believing the hype – in much the same way as Reaganite children once did their "sixties" parents puffing a joint and telling their Woodstock stories again.

The true believers in the spectacle these days are the webmeisters of revolutionary Islam. They are the ones that drink deep, to the point of intoxication, on the spectacle's *derealization* of politics. They are the ones who go on being confident – more and more confident as the years pass – that the virtual life is the road to utopia.

You will gather that we think there are things to fear in the new mutation, and signs of hope. The spectacle is rampant, but at its epicenter less and less persuasive. It accelerates, like capitalism in general, as a result of the falling rate of illusion. The disenchantment of the image-world may follow the disenchantment of the world in general. The spectacle is the key form of social control in present circumstances, but also a source of ongoing instability. The sheer proliferation of image-technology means that too much of the texture of everyday life is captured and circulated, and subject to inflection outside the normal circuits of power. In Boston and Miami, the obscene game show of the election moves to its foreordained conclusion; in Baghdad, the blood of the al-Arabiya reporter splashes, in real time, onto the camera lens.

If the spectacle really is "capital accumulated to the point where it becomes image", then will there also be, at times of crisis like the present, a series of returns to outright image-expropriation? How will the expropriating be done? What will primitive accumulation in the realm of appearances look like? Maybe Allawi's bullying of al-Jazeera will be generalized. If so, does the whole self-defeating apparatus of jamming and petty censorship follow? Will it be TV again *à la* Brezhnev and Ceauçescu?

The crisis is only compounded by the fact of the spectacle's uneven development worldwide. In the spectacular heartland the image-world thins and volatilizes; but out on the consumer frontier it has become one of the key instigators of a new round of Terror and martyrdom. For it offers those newly initiated into its technics *an illusion of political effectiveness* which, in a world of phantasms, may go on seeming enough.

IV

What, in the face of this deadlock, do we hope for from a future movement of opposition? Given that we have been arguing that sooner or later an effective resistance has to be framed in terms that challenge the whole texture of modernity, what do we see as the nodes of such a reworking in the ordinary language of the peace marchers and anti-globalizers?

We see several. There is, for a start, the way opposition to American "bases" – a perfectly standard (and urgent) item of anti-militarism and anti-imperialism – opens more and more onto the whole question of state power. What is a "base", finally, and why does the US want and need to multiply such entities through the known world? We should view the problem through the lens of Guantanamo in particular, as various writers have suggested lately – through what Guantanamo and its satellites make possible, juridically, lawfully/lawlessly. *Bases are the state incarnate*, it soon becomes clear: they embody the state in its extra-territorial sovereignty, its lawmaking and lawbreaking will; the state in its guise of other-directed war machine, but with other-directedness now become other-penetration, -occupation, -infection, -contamination; in the process offering the infected party (the failed state, the subservient social democracy) a positive model of evasion and abrogation of all social constraint.

Bases are a thousand points of darkness: a lymphatic system pumping out antibodies to the rule of law and the remaining (dim) possibility of democratic control. They are a shadow anticipation of the earth as one vast arena of "covert operations" and the "indefinite exercise of extra-legal state power".[148] They are foundational: that is the point. Constitutive of a world in the making. "Base" = Pattern: for the US just as much as for al-Qaida (which has the equation, so we gather, embedded in the very word it chooses for its name).

We build our hopes, in other words, precisely on the enormity of what is challenged when bases are called into question. The challenge in any one case will be local, "national", commonsensical, phrased in a variety of idioms. But the resistance to it, on the part of the sovereign power, will be absolute; and the absolutism of the resistance will itself be a lesson in what bases are, and to what political and economic – not simply military – necessities they answer.

Something of the same could be said, we believe, about various other issues and controversies of the past few years. The challenge to secrecy, for example, is likewise a set of moderate and constitutional arguments – limits, legalities, minimum accountability – and a calling into question of more and more of what the state actually consists of. It is a challenge that has already divided faction from faction within the state apparatus itself. The release of the Abu Ghraib photographs – for all that the exact chain of circumstances leading to the outing is still shrouded in mystery,

---

148 Judith Butler, "Indefinite Detention", in Butler, *Precarious Life: The Powers of Mourning and Violence*, London and New York 2004, p. 64.

and no doubt will remain so – is one among many pieces of evidence lately of a breakdown in the usual media–administration contract. Of course the endless round of inquiries and pointing fingers that followed was in large part for show. But "for show", so this book has been saying, is no longer a fully manipulable dimension of statecraft.

Local challenges, in other words, can escalate into real crises of state confidence. In a parallel way, but even more painfully, the age-old controversy surrounding the bombing of civilians – the legitimacy of Terror from the air and "collateral damage", and the actual *showing* "of Americans and coalition soldiers killing innocent civilians" – is something that leads directly to the question of modernity itself. For *bombing is a constitutive feature of modern life* – now for America too. The experience and preserved memory of blast and firestorm is one of the central strands of twentieth-century identity – in Berlin as much as in Hiroshima, in London as much as (actively now) in Fallujah. Not for nothing will the century go down to posterity – for all the efforts of the US administration – as that of Picasso's *Guernica*. To call back in question the main technics of industrialized warfare, then, is to mobilize the repressed consciousness of modernity's ordinary costs.[149]

There is, in a word, a dimension of totality already there – barely latent – in many of the anti-war movement's images and demands. And if links could be forged between these images and others now occurring every morning in the media – if, for example, the secret world of "contractors" and ex-prison guards and out-of-control security squads in Iraq and Afghanistan could be seen as a necessary facet of the *neo-liberalization of war* – then truly the multitude would be on the verge of naming the enemy. If alongside the man in the hood on our frontispiece could be put the other truly indelible, unforgivable image of the current state of things

---

149 On the repression, see W. G. Sebald, *On the Natural History of Destruction*, New York 2003; and on the costs, Sven Lindqvist, *A History of Bombing*, New York 2001 – two great texts on twentieth-century history.

– the ruined small farmer from South Korea, slashing his arteries in defiance on the barricades at Cancun – then something close to the real outlines of a world of hopelessness and struggle would loom into view.

This last image, which of course we are glad not to show, brings us back finally to the ground – the shifting and terrible ground – for optimism in the present age of darkness. We have painted as grim a picture of the new vanguardism as we knew how, and pointed to the world of misery that such a vanguard is poised to exploit. This was necessary. Al-Qaida is one of modernity's main features. But it is far from being the only one.

V

Over the very same decades in which the new Leninism was assembling its cadres, and in much the same territory – the same fifteen-million-plus cities, the same ruined state system, the same landscape of crash programs and shock therapy and Bhopal-type "friendly investment climates" – a *non*-vanguardist opposition was coming into being. Call it the "movement of movements", call it the struggle against globalization: the terms own up to the still unsettled nature of the new phenomenon – its indelible pluralism, its continual changing of ground and adoption of new tactics, its spontaneity (which does not mean necessarily a simple disconnect from older parties and revolutionary groups), and its lack of interest in scripts of salvation. This is the "multitude" we place most faith in – and precisely *because* its politics depend so little on the new apparatus of spectacle. In this, as in so much else, it is al-Qaida's antithesis.

Even to summon a handful of emblematic instances of the new movement is dangerous, we feel: it risks folding the hiddenness and impermanence of the anti-vanguard into a few bright names – Chiapas, Movimento Sem Terra, Direct Action, the fight against the Narmada hydro-power project in Gujarat, the strikes and sit-ins and sabotage that make a constant descant to the world of sweatshops. But the key point is clear. This opposition – and specifically, this opposition's distance from the vanguard ideal – is as much a product of the present dynamic of capital as any other development of the past quarter-century. Its objects and tactics are a response to the logic of the neo-liberalism it is called on to resist. Capital manifests itself on the movement of movement's terrain as a de-centered, elusive, amoeboid set of temptations and coercions, and therefore has to be confronted in terms just as mobile. Weak states, failed nationalizations, instant speculative raids on currencies, and everywhere the same corporate actors sewing together their worldwide production lines: this is the economic reality the new working classes have grown up with, and whose changing points of vulnerability they go on probing.

Other writers have begun the job of mapping and chronicling this new resistance, and done it with real vividness. We shall not repeat their stories, and we do not claim to know whether finally the pattern of struggles they outline will be enough to stop neo-liberalism in its tracks. (Here as elsewhere, we sit with Satan in hell's fire, still undecided "What reinforcement we may gain from Hope,/If not what resolution from despare".) What we do know is that capitalism, in its present round of primitive accumulation, has encountered a new/old Enemy. And the ground on which battle is joined has something to tell us – us Northerners, us citizens of the spectacular control center – about where and how a practical opposition to modernity might be framed.

Modernity is many things. Secularization is one of them, and speed-up, and the cult of technics, and disenchantment of the world, and false orientation to the future. But right at the heart of capitalist modernity, we would argue, has been a process of endless *enclosure*. The great work of the past half-millennium was the cutting off of the world's natural and human resources from common use. Land, water, the fruits of the forest, the spaces of custom and communal negotiation, the mineral substrate, the life of rivers and oceans, the very airwaves – capitalism has depended, and still depends, on more and more of these shared properties being shared no longer, whatever the violence or absurdity involved in converting the stuff of humanity into this or that item for sale. Enclosure seems to us the best word for the process's overall logic. And it links directly with the new non-vanguard. For what the enemies of neo-liberalism are involved in, centrally, is resistance to attacks on the commons. Capitalism, as the great Karl Polanyi put it half a century ago, is rooted in the continual *disembedding* of basic elements of the species's life-world from the extraordinary matrix of social relations – constraints, understandings, checks and balances, rules of succession, kinds of communal sanction against the exploiter – which had been the central creation of humanity's long history. The disembedding is an atrocity, and will go on being felt as such by those who experience it first hand.

> For the alleged commodity "labor power" cannot be shoved about, used indiscriminately, or even left unused, without affecting also the human individual who happens to be the bearer of this peculiar commodity. In disposing of a man's labor power the system would, incidentally, dispose of the physical, psychological, and moral entity "man" attached to that tag. Robbed of the protective covering of cultural institutions, human beings would perish from the effects of social exposure; they would die as the victims of acute social dislocation through vice, perversion, crime, and starvation. Nature would be reduced to its elements, neighborhoods and landscapes defiled, rivers polluted, military safety jeopardized [sic], the power to produce food and raw materials destroyed.[150]

---

150   Karl Polanyi, *The Great Transformation: The Political and Economic Origins of Our Time*, Boston 1957 (first pub. 1944), p. 73. Writing in 1944, Polanyi was convinced that the disasters of the previous fifteen years would convince capital, once and for all, that the social and human cost of this disembedding was too high. His optimism was his only mistake.

Some of the language here has dated. But in almost every respect it remains – more and more – a text for the times.

It may even be that the concept of enclosure, and the question of effective tactics in opposition to it, will serve as a lens through which North and South will come to recognize – for all their differences, which it would be foolish to conjure away – a degree of common ground. For the North too is victim of a new round of disembedding and crude bids for exclusive ownership. The bio-prospectors fan out across the genetic hinterland, looking for the stuff of life to patent and manipulate; the giant proprietors of radio frequencies call on the state to guarantee – to intensify – their monopoly of speech; the apparatus of basic public services, won from the long struggles of the twentieth century, is to be starved of resources and sold off cheap; there is to be a worldwide market in permits to pollute; the very *germplasm* is to be commodified.

We are realists. We recognize that the sheer enormity of this new round of enclosure has so far made awareness of it, and resistance to it, fitful. It is hard to bring into focus, hard to demystify. But resistance does exist, and is intensifying; and once again, the fact of war brings many things into sharper relief. "McDonald's cannot flourish without McDonnell Douglas …. And the hidden fist that keeps the world safe for Silicon Valley's technologies to flourish is called the US Army, Navy, Air Force, and Marine Corps."[151] When capitalism itself is obliged to utter these home truths (however smugly, however confident the writer in his well-informed readers' assent) then truly the terms of engagement have changed. Military neo-liberalism is revealed as such.

"When we affect to pity as poor those who must labor or the world cannot exist, we are trifling with the condition of mankind." Thus Edmund Burke. We take this still to be the common wisdom of our masters. To it might be added the words of one of Bush's advisers

151 Thomas Friedman, *New York Times Magazine*, March 28, 1999.

recently, assessing the spectacle from his special vantage point: "We are an empire now, and when we act, we create our own reality."[152]

It is the voice of absolutism through the ages; only now in possession of an unprecented machinery to make its wishes the world. And against it, finally, only Milton will do. "And reassembling our afflicted Powers,/ Consult how we may henceforth most offend/Our Enemy …". Till, maybe

> … Somewhere at some new moon,
> We'll learn that sleeping is not death.
> Hearing the whole earth change its tune,
> Its flesh being wild, and it again
> Crying aloud …[153]

The crying is audible, and the earth begins to shake off sleep.

---

152   Quoted in Ron Suskind, "Without a Doubt", *New York Times Magazine*, October 17, 2004.
153   W. B. Yeats, "At Galway Races", *The Green Helmet and Other Poems*, Dundrum 1910.

AFTERWORD

The following is an exchange that took place in the autumn of 2005 between the authors of *Afflicted Powers* and Hal Foster for the editors of the journal *October*.

Q. *"The distinctive feature of the new world situation," you write early on, is "its deep and perplexing doubleness ... A bald-faced imperialism is crossed with a struggle for control of 'information'." And later you sum up: "Primitive accumulation is to be carried out in conditions of spectacle: that is the new reality in a nutshell."*

Yet how new, finally, is this reality, how distinctive this doubleness? However extreme it appears today, isn't the conjunction of "atavism and newfangledness" structural to the dialectic of modernization at large? That is, are we witness to a shift in degree or in kind here?

Retort. If we immediately have recourse to a quote from Brecht, will that confirm the question's implicit suspicions? (When in doubt, wheel out the quizzical Stalinist one more time ...)

Perhaps. But we cannot help feeling that the poem below speaks more completely to the "dialectic of modernization" than anything we have seen since. It is the first of Brecht's *Five Visions* from 1938, called "Parade of the Old New." ("Parade" makes a welcome change from "spectacle,"

---

1   A somewhat different version of this interview appeared in *October* 115, Winter 2006.

which is a word, we realize, that gets a bit shopworn and all-consuming
with time.)

> I stood on a hill and I saw the Old approaching, but it came as the New.
>   It hobbled up on new crutches which no one had ever seen before
> and stank of new smells of decay which no one had ever smelt.
>   The stone that rolled past was the newest invention and the screams
> of the gorillas drumming on their chests set up to be the newest thing
> in music.
>   Everywhere you could see open graves standing empty as the New
> advanced on the capital.
>   Round about stood those who inspire terror, shouting: Here comes
> the New, it's all new, salute the New, be new like us! And those who
> heard, heard nothing but their shouts, but those who saw, saw certain
> people who were not shouting.
>   So the Old strode in disguised as the New, but it brought the New
> with it in its triumphal procession and presented it as the Old.
>   The New went fettered and in rags. They revealed its splendid limbs.
>   And the procession moved through the night, but what they thought
> was the light of dawn was the light of fires in the sky. And the cry: Here
> comes the New, it's all new, salute the New, be new like us! would have been
> easier to hear if everything had not been drowned in the thunder of guns.

This sounds like the world we live in.

We agree with you, and with Brecht, that there is never an end in
modernity to the swapping of places between atavism and newfangledness. This is because atavism is modernity's truth. Modernity is a
mutation of the Old. Its newness is not structural. Everything about the
basic furnishing of human oppression and misery has remained
unchanged in the last 150 years – except that the machinery has been
speeded up, and various ameliorations painted in on top. The New that

modernity offers is never, and can never be, the kind of rethinking and reconstruction of our productive and symbol-making powers that would again put past and future in genuine dialogue. "Newfangled" is a late-medieval word, which from the start had no illusions about the kind of novelty markets have to offer.

Nonetheless we do think there is something distinctive about the Old New of the past four years. *Afflicted Powers* is an attempt to describe it. Very roughly, what seems to us unprecedented is the starkness – the extremity – of the confrontation between New Oldness and Old Newness. No one, surely, came close to anticipating that the opening of the 21st century would be structured around a battle between two such virulently reactionary forms of world power (or will to world power), and that both sides would see so clearly that the battle is now to be fought by *both* bombs (crude attempts at re-colonization, old-time resistance struggles, patient recruitment of armed cadres, crowds waving the latest version of the Little Red Book) and images.

Q. *The 9/11 terrorists, you write, "followed the logic of the spectacle to its charnel-house conclusion." Yet you also credit them with great strategic canniness, anticipating that the "perpetual emotion machines" could be "captured for a moment" to produce "the perfect image of capitalism's negation," and that the US response would be to lash out, militarily, and so "confirm the world of Islam in its despairing strength."*

Is the spectacle as calculable in its consequences as you suggest here? Was 9/11 so foreseeable in its effects – both in "the West" and throughout the Islamic world? You acknowledge that "the new terrorists succumbed to the temptation of the spectacle"; at times in your text might you do so as well – to the temptation, above all, of its semblance of totality? Granted, you speak of its complex appearance and uneven development around the globe (even as it now achieves global reach); yet might your use of the concept sometimes occlude other forces – of power and opposition alike – and drive other critical models of both prematurely out of court? Has the state truly come "to live and die by its investment in, and control of, the field of images"? Isn't this – might the very concept of the spectacle be – a somewhat paranoid formulation which reduces the possibility of effective opposition to power?

Retort. Bombs and images. If we were to point to a basic disagreement we have with the overall drift of your questions, it would center on your suggestion that really in the book – or at key moments in the book – it is the image-world and the image-battle that are primary. This suggestion seems to single out and focus on our Chapters 1 and 6, where the nature of spectacle and modernity is tackled head on. We do not claim to have solved the problem – the intractable problem, which seems to us the main theoretical challenge to Left politics in the present – of thinking the technics and dynamics of the struggle for mastery in the realm of appearance in relation to the more familiar, and newly visible, facts of imperial power. But this is what the book tries to do; this is the task it sets itself. So that even in the chapter which takes as its object the spectacular dimension of the past four years of international politics, it is predominantly the spectacle as a form of state power – the state's entrapment in the logic of image-control, and the possible vulnerabilities such entrapment brings in its wake – that concerns us. Even the notion we propose of September 11 as a moment of image-defeat, which is as close as we come to entertaining the idea that the field of disseminated appearances may now be seen as a specific political terrain, with its own determinant weight in the equation of interests and material capacities; even this immediately opens onto a discussion of what it was – in the actual availability of armed force, and the lack of effective imperial control of client regimes – that September 11 brought into focus.

Perhaps we should say it explicitly: it may or may not be the case that a particular image-event can *in itself* alter the balance of world-political forces, surging out of the blue of international disorder and remaking the terms of statecraft. Logically this is possible. The notion of spectacle at least suggests a tendential development toward a situation in which, empirically, something like this might one day happen. *But September 11 was not it.* It was an image-defeat, yes; but it only produced the long-term or mid-term effects that it did because, as an image, it resonated so ominously with the gross material realities of "failed states," the disintegrating world arms market, the threats to the state's monopoly of the means of mass destruction, and the general neo-liberalization of war.

This much is stated in the chapter itself. And we defend and reassert here the notion that Chapter 1 of *Afflicted Powers* – the discussion of spectacle – stands in complex relation to the chapters that follow. We meant it when we said in the book that "[n]o one level of analysis – 'economic' or 'political,' global or local, focusing on the means of either material or symbolic production – will do justice to the current mixture of chaos and grand design." Or again, at the end of the Introduction, that "[r]eaders will find themselves shifting, in the chapters that follow, between hard and disagreeable materialities – cold figures of profit, piled-up statistics of death and impoverishment – and broadranging speculation on current forms of social control. This double perspective is true to the nature of the moment."

We are painfully aware that much of the work of coordinating our terms of analysis – plotting spectacle against primitive accumulation as the two imperatives actually collide, or specifying the year-by-year tensions in state policy between the logic of permanent militarization and the necessities of "weak citizenship" – remains to be done. But *some* of it we do in the book. The discussion of spectacle, for instance, makes no sense without the picture of state power sketched in "Permanent War." "Blood for Oil?" is in high tension with "Permanent War," and meant to be. The chapters rehearse two logics of imperialism, and do not claim to be able to map the one onto the other at all precisely. (We shall go on trying. Some such map, we are convinced, is what the anti-war movement needs.) The chapter on Israel is, among other things, an attempt to point to a case in which a "spectacular" relation between states, as opposed to one based on more normal calculations of global interest, has had specific effects. The survey of modernity in Chapter 6 (whose risks we acknowledge in the text) is prepared for, we hope, by the account of Qutb and al-Qaida that precedes it.

And so on. This acknowledgement of what we were unable to do in the book is not *pro forma*. From start to finish of the project we were haunted by the fear that the very disparity of our terms of analysis would in the end stand in the way of effective totalization. (This for us would be a defect – at least in a text that aims to describe the main lines of international politics – not a thing to be proud of.) But we saw no way out of the dilemma. The heterogeneity of our terms was true to the facts.

Above all – and here is where we find this set of questions sometimes a bit dispiriting – we wanted to find ways of taking spectacle seriously as a term of political explanation without turning it into the key to all mysteries. In a word, the concept needed to be *desacralized*. It needed to be applied, locally and conjuncturally – to dirty its hands with the details of politics. We wanted *Afflicted Powers* to start from the premise (which we saw confirmed month by month by the whole dynamic of the Iraq disaster) that the spectacle is subject, like everything else, to change, and is not necessarily able to assimilate every challenge, every destabilization. *An image-world can enter into crisis* – as we believe has happened since September 2001. Saying so does not entail any final verdict on the crisis's depth, or the long-term danger it poses to the apparatus of spectacular symbol-management. The crisis may be temporary. But it is a crisis. Over the past four years the world of appearances has been, to some degree, reconstellated. That we recognize the ability of the image-apparatus to recuperate this moment of openness – that we even acknowledge that "crisis" is a repeated trope of spectacle itself, always flashing up the doom and fascination of "modernity" in some anguished new shape on the screen – again says nothing against the need to describe those forces that lately put spectacle in doubt.

Q. *"Ultimately," you write, "the spectacle comes out of a barrel of a gun. State power informs and enforces it. Mostly that fact is hidden. The spectacle is that hiding."*

Here your doubles – primitive accumulation and spectacle, "the military neo-liberalism" of the imperial US and "the perpetual emotion machines" of the media – suddenly become one. "Unless I am very mistaken," Adorno wrote, snootily enough, to Benjamin regarding his "Arcades" project, "your dialectic lacks one thing: media-tion." Might some of your own readers be similarly "mistaken" – especially given passages like this one where the spectacle is both mediated and mediator? "Is this a 'material'," Adorno also asks Benjamin, "which can patiently await inter-pretation without being consumed by its own aura?" Might your account of this doubleness have a related kind of magical force – or is this unmediated yoking together of extremes part of "the magic" of the current regime, its transgression of once-accepted limits of power that seems to spellbind so many? Yet if so, might you rehearse this magic in your very description of it (as Marx, it might be argued, fetishizes the commodity in his very account)?

Retort. "Ultimately, the spectacle comes out of the barrel of a gun." We think we understand your uneasiness here. But don't take our *détournement* of Mao too literally. Really all our Little Red aphorism says is the obvious: that insofar as the spectacle of social order presents itself now as a constant image-flow of contentment, obedience, enterprise, and unifor-mity it is, equally constantly, guaranteed by the exercise of state power. Necessarily so, since contentment, obedience, enterprise, and uniformity involve the suppression of their opposites, which the actual structure and texture of everyday life reproduce – intensify – just as fast as the spectacle assures us they are things of the past. We are not quite clear why saying so strikes you as collapsing the one form of social control into the other. Of course we are interested in occasions at which such a collapse actually happens, precipitated by historical events. Remember that our post-Maoist cliché comes at the end of a chapter on Israel. The armored bulldozers thirty feet high, the Tim Burton neatness of the strategic suburbs, the rubble of the Gaza ideal homes, the constant clatter of the helicopter gunships, the gray of the turrets along the separation wall, looking out on the filth of No Man's Land … We are with Benjamin, against Adorno, in believing that history at moments *consumes* mediation, and puts the obscenity of power naked on stage.

Q. *You draw your title from Book I of* Paradise Lost *– the "afflicted powers" are those of Satan cast down. And even here, in affliction, there is a doubleness in your analysis: the Left is afflicted (who could argue?), yet, you insist, so is the imperial US. In fact you term 9/11 "a spectacular defeat" for this regime, claiming it has "no answer to [the] image victory" of al-Qaida: "Where, in the end, is the image the war machine has been looking for – the one to put paid to the September haunting?" And as you note, the most infamous image to circulate since 9/11 – that of the hooded torture victim at Abu Ghraib – "instantly dismantled the rhetoric of liberation."*

With defeats like these, some in D.C. backrooms and bars might chuckle, who needs victories? As you also suggest, 9/11 has served as the cover both for the military neoliberalism prosecuted abroad and for the political neoliberalism pursued at home – less a frantic "reassembling" of powers, perhaps, than an awesome burgeoning of them. (And no doubt for some Pentagon people Abu Ghraib has its use-value as well.) "Why," you ask, "should we follow the lead of the spectacle itself in electing this one among many atrocities … as a world-historical turning point?" Why indeed? Doesn't your affirmation of the putatively epochal status of 9/11 play into the ideology of John "Our Lives Were Forever Changed" Ashcroft et al.? Or, if 9/11 was indeed a defeat, might it be a momentary one on the order of "the culture of defeat" á la Wolfgang Schivelbush – a national trauma quickly transformed into an imperial triumphalism?

Retort. "With defeats like these, who needs victories?" We guess this is essentially the Carl Schmitt challenge: that in practice September 11 gave the US state the classic opportunity it is always looking for, to reorient politics around the "us and them"/ "friend and enemy" distinction that is the state's eternal alibi. (There is a Conspiracy Hillbilly version of this, which we leave to the attentions of the mice …) The challenge is interesting, but the actual pattern of events does not seem to us to have followed the Schmittian script very closely. If the last two years have been (covert) victory for the state, what would defeat look like? States certainly can thrive on the "construction" of an enemy, but not if the enemy turns out to be actually victorious in the field. The cunning of reason can only go so far. Handing Iraq on a plate to the mullahs, or at least – by the combination of its hubris and incapacity – both enraging and emboldening to active resistance huge numbers of people across the Islamic world, seems a high price to pay for unanimity (and Republican votes) at home. And what unanimity? For how long? The trouble with the spectacle, from the state's point of view, is that its monadology of consumption constantly dissolves (even paranoid) distinctions and puts Don't Know in their place.

Q. *In the last few decades "Situationism" has been often (ab)used as a rhetorical way to shore up some "illusion of political effectiveness" (as you put it in another context). We imagine you are more than skeptical of this tendency (indeed, not long ago* October *published a text, coauthored by one of your party, with the title "Why Art Can't Kill the Situationist International?"). But you have little to say in* Afflicted Powers *about art, or indeed of culture, that is not one with the spectacle. In your analysis is this space now voided?*

Retort. "In your analysis is this space now voided?" Analytically, of course it cannot be. Empirically, we wonder who's been doing the voiding.

This morning's (2 September 2005) newspapers, at least in the US, featured the following words from Mohammad Sidique Khan, one of the London bombers – spoken with a south Yorkshire accent, we are told, so if the video is an al-Qaida concoction they have, as usual, been working hard at the details of visual reality:

> I am going to keep this short and to the point because it's all been said by far more eloquent people than me. But our words have no impact upon you. Therefore I'm going to talk to you in a language that you understand. Our words are dead until we give them life with our blood.
>
> I'm sure by now the media has painted a suitable picture of me. This predictable propaganda machine will naturally try to put a spin on it to suit the government and to scare the masses into conforming to their power- and wealth-obsessed agendas.
>
> I and thousands like me are forsaking everything for what we believe. Our driving motivation doesn't come from tangible commodities that this world has to offer.
>
> This is how our ethical stances are dictated: Your democratically elected governments continuously perpetuate atrocities against my people, and your support of them makes you directly responsible, just as I am directly responsible for protecting and avenging my Muslim brothers and sisters.
>
> Until we feel security, you will be our target. Until you stop the bombing, gassing, imprisonment and torture of my people, we will not stop this fight. We are at war and I am a soldier. Now you too will taste the reality of this situation.

This, sadly, is the voice of our time. It is the New Old speaking. Of course it is possible for art to reply even to this extremity – did we not start our set of answers with a prose-poem by Brecht? And does it not still apply, all too vividly? Do we not begin *Afflicted Powers* by putting Milton opposite Abu Ghraib? And by describing the Bush administration's panic in the face of *Guernica*?

But we look around at the actually existing artworld of the Empire and see no reason to expect much in the same vein. We shall ask readers to put alongside Mohammad Sidique Khan's last testament a listing of the themes and styles of this week's gallery offerings in New York and London, or wherever the readers are, or a sample of the "ethical stances" of their reviewers, and judge for themselves.

Q. *"Modernity" appears as an unmitigated horror in your text ("war is modernity incarnate," you write at one point). We make no apologies for modernity (much less offer lessons in dialectics), but is it as utterly disastrous as you make it out to be?*

Your stark definition of modernity forces you into sheer opposition to it, and this position seems to draw you into a relation of enemy-twinship with revolutionary Islam, a relation from which you then struggle to escape. "How we may henceforth most offend our enemy" – you share Satan's lines with al-Qaida, and yet, even as you too are horrified by Osama and company, and even as you deliver a blistering critique of vanguardism, you show a begrudging respect for this "vanguard of Terror": "the new vanguard has been able to take advantage of the new world order in ways that have left most other forms of opposition far behind." More than once you call for "an opposition to modernity having nothing in common with al-Qaida's … non-orthodox, non-nostalgic, non-rejectionist, non-apocalyptic." Yet here you seemed to be locked in an oppositionality that you can't quite spring open.

Might it be today that radical invention, and not only reckless power, is most in the hands of the Right – both here and abroad?

Retort. "Might it be today that radical invention is most in the hands of the Right?" In many ways it seems so – and not for the first time in the last 100 years. (We are back to Brecht in 1938 again.)

This connects with your unease, several times repeated in your questions to us, at the vehemence of *Afflicted Powers'* hostility to modernity as such. The issues here are complex, but essentially we stick to our guns. It is possible, we believe, to approach the phenomena of modernity from a position of root-and-branch opposition and yet generate the best, most adequate, descriptions of what it is one opposes. It is not only possible, it seems in practice to be *necessary*. To describe modernity, one has to think (and feel) culturally, anthropologically – one has to keep at the center of one's sense of things modernity's disorienting, disenchanting power. And never lose hold of the extremity of that disenchantment, as it is lived by actual human subjects finding (and losing) their way in a new form of life.

This is why the critique and assessment of modernity has come so often and so powerfully from Fascists, Maurassians, Anglo-Catholics, and assorted psychopomps. And why the Left, with its eternal "hard-headedness" and optimism in the face of the new (Old) technics, has so utterly failed to get modernity in its sights. It is possible, further, to approach the current mutations of modernity from a position of utter loathing without for a moment believing that modernity is reversible – without orienting one's opposition on a fantasy of Going Back. The Right's radicalism is the radicalism of Return. But there will be no Return. What, then, will the Left's radicalism be premised on? Not on the promise of cyberspace, we hope. Not on an empty *Avanti!*

You are right that in calling on the Left to sketch out a new form of opposition to the modern – one having nothing in common with the warring fundamentalisms – the best we can do in the book is intimate what that new form will have *not* to be. "Non-orthodox, non-nostalgic, non-rejectionist, non-apocalyptic," etc. We agree this gets us only to the start of things. But even to get to the start – even to propose the reconstruction of the critique of modernity as now the Left's main theoretical task – is something, in the state of utter intellectual nullity at present characteristic of opposition forces in the US (with their endless policy studies plus futile sniping at Bush).

Let us say it again. For a mixture of good and bad reasons, the critique of modernity over the past 100 years or so – as opposed to the critique of capitalism – came most powerfully from the Right. The Left had no patience for the critique's foundation in nostalgia (so-called), organicism, High Romantic individualism, and aristocratic disdain for mass culture and slave *ressentiment*. The impatience was justified, but the result of the Left's abstention from the question of modernity was in the end disastrous. It ceded the ground of anger and fear and disorientation in face of the "all that is solid" to a cruel and resourceful foe. So that simply to pose the question, "What would a non-aristocratic, non-reactionary opposition to modernity be like?" is immediately to feel a rhetorical – and even more, a conceptual – void opening beneath one's feet. There is, to be sure, a post-Commune tradition rejecting modernity's theatrics of representation. But with science now harnessed full-time to the project of capital, the 19th-century opposition – not least Kropotkin and the anti-authoritarian Left – lies revealed as impeccably modern in its scientism. And to the extent that the 20th century's Left tradition did include moments when the modern condition was thought about whole – as of course was true of Benjamin and Adorno, or, for that matter, of Debord and Lefebvre – what resulted most often, it seems now in retrospect, was Right-wing motifs repeated in an ultra-Left register.

We are now living through a new round of resistance to modernity – a globalized guerrilla, as we say in the book, making at last the "ten, twenty, a hundred Vietnams" that Che called for a generation ago. Little did he dream in whose name, and in favor of what, the new insurgencies would be fought! And little did he realize how defenceless the Left's metaphysics would leave it – the Left's compound of cheery technophilia and communitarian humanism, we mean – in the face of a true *demonization* of the life-world capitalism had brought into being. Modernity, says

Benjamin somewhere in the Arcades Project, is "the time of Hell." The language, again, is that of the Right. It is a line from the Pisan *Cantos*. We could imagine it nowadays issuing straight from al-Zawahiri's mouth. But what *other* imagery, what other rhetoric, what other set of descriptions might be possible – ones that find form for the horror and emptiness of the modern, but *hold out no promise of Going Back* – seems to us the political question of the years to come.

ENDNOTE

Afflicted Powers has its origins in an anti-war broadsheet called *Neither Their War Nor Their Peace*, but its impetus also springs from a Retort gathering in February 2003, at which we discussed with Perry Anderson his essay "Force and Consent" (*New Left Review* 17, Sept/Oct 2002). Four who were in the company that evening took up the task of turning the broadsheet into a pamphlet (which in the event became this book). The collaboration depended on an ongoing critical dialogue within Retort, and on Retort's sustaining web of friendship and camaraderie. We have some special debts of gratitude to acknowledge: to Ann Banfield, Amita Baviskar, Gillian Boal, Jim Brook, Terry Burke, Michael Klare, Peter Linebaugh, Paul Lubeck, Donald Nicholson-Smith, Mary Beth Pudup, and Eddie Yuen for help along the way, and particularly to Anne Wagner for her immensely helpful reading of the complete manuscript. We thank Ed Kashi for his photographs, and Lara Adler at the Corbis Agency for help with the gathering of images. And the whole beast was put into consistent formal order with the assistance of Jason Strange.

What follows is a brief bibliographic prompt – in no way meant to be comprehensive – for readers interested in pursuing the main themes of *Afflicted Powers*.

Introduction

In assembling 131 photographs from thirty cities worldwide, *2/15: The Day the World Said No to War* (Barbara Sauermann ed., Edinburgh 2003) catches the spirit of the global demonstrations on the eve of the Iraq war. Reaction on the Left to Michael Hardt and Antoni Negri's *Empire* (Cambridge 2002) and *Multitude* (London 2004) has been strangely deferential. For an exception, see Timothy Brennan, "The Empire's New Clothes", *Critical Inquiry*, Winter 2003.

The State, the Spectacle, and September 11

For the original expositions of the concepts of spectacle and the colonization of everyday life, see Guy Debord, *Society of the Spectacle*, trans. Donald Nicholson-Smith (New York 1994) [orig. pub. 1967] and Guy Debord, *Comments on the Society of the Spectacle*, trans. Malcolm Imrie (London 1998) [orig. pub. 1988]. For further discussion and application of the concepts, see Raoul Vaneigem, *The Revolution of Everyday Life*, trans. Donald Nicholson-Smith (London 1994), Ken Knabb, ed., *Situationist International Anthology* (Berkeley 1981), and Anselm Jappé, *Guy Debord* (London 1999).

Blood for Oil?

Michael Klare lays out the blood-for-oil thesis clearly in *Blood and Oil: The Dangers and Consequences of America's Growing Petroleum Dependency* (New York 2004). The end-of-oil debate is explored in David Goodstein, *Out of Gas* (New York 2004), and at www.princeton.edu/hubbert/current-events.html, www.peakoil.net, and www.hubbertpeak.com. The best political economy of global oil is Jonathan Nitzan and Shimshon Bichler, *The Global Political Economy of Israel* (London 1999). The texture of life amid petro-excess is well conveyed in the trilogy of novels by (ex-oil man) Abdelrahman Munif, *Cities of Salt* (New York 1978). On the relations between oil and primitive accumulation *Midnight Oil* (Brooklyn 1992) by the Midnight Notes Collective is foundational. The best account of corruption and oil states appears in Catholic Relief Service's "Bottom of the Barrel" 2003 (www.catholicrelief.org/africanoil.cfm). More generally, the relations between primitive accumulation and capitalism are charted in Michael Perelman's *The Invention of Capitalism* (Chapel Hill 2001) and David Harvey's *The New Imperialism* (London 2003). Peter Gowan's *The Global Gamble* (London 2000) and Robert Brenner's *The Economics of Global Turbulence* (London 2005) are primers on the rise of neo-liberalism and its relation to American economic power. On the crisis of secular nationalism see Timothy Mitchell, *The Rule of Experts* (Berkeley 2002) and Partha Chatterjee, *The Nation and its Fragments* (Princeton 1993). Karl Polanyi's *The Great Transformation* (Boston 1944) is classic. The ideas of Polanyi are powerfully applied to the crisis of US hegemony in Giovanni Arrighi and Beverly Silver's "Polanyi's Double Movement", *Politics and Society*, vol. 31, no. 2, 2003, pp. 325–55.

Permanent War

From the spate of recent books on American empire, two demonstrate its consistency over time: Chalmers Johnson's *The Sorrows of Empire: Militarism, Secrecy, and the End of the Republic* (New York 2004) and, from the Right, Andrew J. Bacevich's *American Empire: The Realities and Consequences of US Diplomacy* (Cambridge 2002). In the formidable list of Noam Chomsky's publications on the subject, his *American Power and the New Mandarins* (New York 1969) never ceases to be relevant. Diana Johnstone offers a clear-eyed analysis of the Balkans disaster in *Fools' Crusade: Yugoslavia, NATO and Western Delusions* (New York 2002). On the long and underchronicled history of pacification through state terror from the air, see Susan Griffin's *A Chorus of Stones* (New York 1992) and Sven Lindqvist's *A History of Bombing* (New York 2000).

The Future of an Illusion

The early history of the relationship between the US state and Zionism is laid out in Peter Grose's *Israel in the Mind of America* (New York 1983). The post-1945 relationship, including the dynamics of the pro-Israel lobby, is well excavated by Cheryl A. Rubenberg in *Israel and the American National Interest* (Urbana and Chicago 1986). Christian fundamentalist support for Zionism is aired in Ruth W. Mouly's "Israel's Christian Comforters and Critics", in *Anti-Zionism: Analytical Reflections,* edited by R. Tekiner, S. Abed-Rabbo, and N. Mezvinsky (Brattleboro 1988). Tanya Rinehart's *Israel/Palestine* (New York 2002) exposes the fraud of the Oslo and Camp David accords. As to the specifics of US support for the Israeli state during the Cold War, Noam Chomsky's *The Fateful Triangle: The United States, Israel, and the Palestinians* (Boston 1983) remains a basic text.

Revolutionary Islam

Edward Said's *Orientalism* (New York 1978) is still essential. Malise Ruthven's *Islam: A Very Short Introduction* (Oxford 1997) is what it says, and a good one. On the relations between Islam and the secular see Talal Asad, *Formations of the Secular* (Stanford 2003). Al-Azmeh's *Islams and Modernities* (London 1996) and Mahmood Mamdani's *Good Muslim, Bad Muslim* (New York 2004) provide powerful analyses of the rise of political Islam in the modern world. Elizabeth Euben's *Enemy in the Mirror* (Princeton 1999) gives a political theorist's view of revolutionary Islam and of the work of Qutb in particular, while Gilles Kepel, *The War for Muslim Minds* (Harvard 2004) and Olivier Roy, *Globalized Islam* (New York 2004) provide exemplary treatments of Islamism and globalization. On

Saudi Arabia and its relation to global Islamism, As'ad Abukhalil's *The Battle for Saudi Arabia* (New York 2004), Timothy Mitchell, "McJihad: Islam in the US Global order", *Social Text*, vol. 73, no. 20, 2002, pp. 1–18, and the International Crisis Group's publications (www.icg.org) stand out. On al-Qaida and other revolutionary cells, Steve Coll's *Ghost Wars* (London 2003) and John Cooley's *Unholy Wars* (London 2000) are very useful. But the best way to grasp the vitality of internal debate over, and within, modern Islam is to visit sites such as www.islamonline.net, www.islamtoday.net, www.muslimworld.org, and www.islamcity.com. For coverage of the insurgency in Iraq, see Professor Juan Cole's website: www.juancole.com.

Modernity and Terror

Among the mass of literature on consumerism, we have learnt most from Arjun Appadurai, *The Social Life of Things: Commodities in Cultural Perspective* (Cambridge 1986), Ben Fine and Ellen Leopold, *The World of Consumption* (London and New York 1993), N. McKendrick et al., *The Birth of a Consumer Society: The Commercialization of Eighteenth-Century England* (London 1982), and the pioneering small book by Judith Williamson, *Decoding Advertisements: Ideology and Meaning in Advertising* (London 1978) – a subject that needs revisiting. The anti-globalization movement and key debates within it are best documented in Eddie Yuen et al., *Confronting Capitalism: Dispatches from a Global Movement* (New York 2004). Also very useful are David McNally, *Another World is Possible* (Winnipeg 2004) and Tom Mertes, ed., *A Movement of Movements* (London 2004). On the early enclosures and their consequences in the transition to capitalism, see Silvia Federici's *Caliban and the Witch* (Brooklyn 2004). For discussion of the new enclosures, *Midnight Notes* #10, Fall 1990, is the essential starting point; Massimo De Angelis's *The Commoner*, on-line at www.thecommoner.org, has become a great resource.

INDEX